RADHIKA HOWARTH

FLAVOURS
WITHOUT BORDERS

80 DISHES CONNECTING CULTURES AND CUISINES

FLAVOURS
WITHOUT BORDERS

First edition printed in 2024 in the UK

ISBN: 978-1-915538-32-1

Written by: Radhika Howarth

@radikalkitchen

Edited by: Emily Readman & Phil Turner

Recipe photography by: Paul Gregory
(www.paulgregoryphotography.co.uk)

Location photography: Vanshita Udayan,
Bhavuk Vishnoi & Namesh Garg

Designed by: Paul Cocker

Sales: Emma Toogood

Contributors: Cara Snowden, Ben Doyle
& Sophia Derby

Hamilton Beach

Published by Meze Publishing Limited
Unit 1b, 2 Kelham Square
Kelham Riverside
Sheffield S3 8SD
Web: www.mezepublishing.co.uk
Telephone: 0114 275 7709
Email: info@mezepublishing.co.uk

Printed by: Bell & Bain Ltd, Glasgow, UK

FOREWORD

When my daughter Radhika approached me about writing a foreword for her book, Flavours Without Borders, I was filled with pride and joy. This book is not just a collection of recipes, but a beautiful journey through a world of flavours, spices, and colours that will excite foodies from all corners of the globe.

Radhika has always had a passion for exploring different cuisines and understanding the stories behind them. In Flavours Without Borders, she has meticulously traced the journey of various ingredients from their countries of origin to their integration into local cuisines around the world. The result is a series of simple yet dynamic recipes that highlight how the same ingredient can create diverse dishes, each with their own unique flavour and texture.

What makes this book truly special is its concept and the stories it shares. Radhika has not only provided delicious recipes but has also shown how food connects us and how flavours can bind us together, regardless of our backgrounds. Her recipes are simple enough for anyone to try, yet they are bursting with flavours that will leave a lasting impression.

As a mother, it has been a joy to see her passion for food and flavours grow over the years. Radhika's dedication to tracing the journey of food and sharing it with the world is truly commendable. This book is a testament to her hard work, creativity, and love for bringing people together through food.

I give her full credit for writing this book, whose dishes truly represent flavours without borders. Wishing her all the best and good luck in this wonderful endeavour.

I am confident that Flavours Without Borders will inspire you to try new recipes, explore new flavours, and appreciate the rich tapestry of global cuisine. Savour the journey, and may these recipes bring joy and connection to your table, just as they have to ours.

With love and pride,

Ma - Shamoli Chatterjee Seth

CONTENTS

MY HEARTFELT THANKS

Writing this book has been a dream come true. I have always wanted to capture and share my passion for flavours, my love for cooking, and my enthusiasm for exploring cuisines from around the world. This book is the first milestone in my culinary adventures; a nirvana moment for me that has allowed me to share my passion for flavours and bring my favourite recipes to life.

I want to say a big thank you and express my heartfelt gratitude to a few people who have made this journey possible and brought me so much happiness.

MY PUBLISHING TEAM

I want to start by saying thank you to **Phil Turner**, Director at Meze Publishing, for believing in me. I still remember my first phone call with him when I was in India, confidently telling him that my concept was the most unique and best in the world. Thank you for trusting in me and my ideas, and for helping me refine the original concept of *Flavours Without Borders* to make it what it is today.

Paul Cocker, thank you for the incredible thought and effort you put into designing the book. I deeply appreciate your patience with my numerous design requests. Thank you for your commitment to designing a book that beautifully conveys the lively spirit and enthusiasm of Radikal Kitchen, while also capturing the emotional elements that make it so personal. You have created a wonderful tribute to my mother, and for that, I am incredibly grateful.

Emma Toogood, thank you for everything you have done to promote the book. I am so grateful for your guidance and support throughout this process. Your energy and enthusiasm were truly uplifting, and I really appreciate all your efforts to showcase my book to the world.

Paul Gregory, thank you for bringing my food to life with your stunning photographs; I loved our intense sessions of food styling and photography. You are a magician.

Emily Readman, thank you for your meticulous and patient editing. I truly appreciate you asking just the right questions to ensure the culinary histories were engaging and insightful. You are brilliant!

HAMILTON BEACH UK

Thank you, **Harry Singh**, Managing Director of Hamilton Beach UK, for your generous support and sponsorship. Your contribution has been invaluable, and I truly appreciate your help in making this project a success!

MY PHOTOGRAPHERS IN INDIA

A big thank you to **Vanshita Udayan** and **Bhavuk Vishnoi** in New Delhi and **Namesh Garg** in Gwalior for beautifully capturing the energy, fun, emotion, and vibrancy of India in every shot.

MY SCHOOL

Thank you, **Mrs. Nishi Mishra**, for your time and for allowing me to capture my cherished school memories. I am forever indebted to my school and the staff at Scindia Kanya Vidyalaya for shaping me into the person I am today.

MY CULINARY CONTRIBUTORS

Thank you to my most wonderful friends for sharing your incredible recipes in this book. I am truly grateful for your generosity in sharing not just your culinary expertise, but also some treasured family recipes. Your contributions have immensely enhanced the authenticity and richness of this collection, and I couldn't have done it without you.

My heartfelt thanks to:

Ademar Neto – Granny's Fish Moqueca from Brazil (see page 86)

Alireza Sarrafan – Zereshk Polo ba Morgh from Iran (see page 42)

Bina Mehta – Mombasa Coconut Chutney from Kenya (see page 204)

Janet Noad - Coronation Chicken from the United Kingdom (see page 74)

Janti Dugal – Tante Noni's Vegetable Coconut Stew from Indonesia (see page 202)

Reiko Hashimoto – Reiko's Dengaku Tofu from Japan (see page 68)

Roshini Karunatilleke – Devilled Prawns from Sri Lanka (see page 92)

Vitor Lopes – Bacalhau à Brás from Portugal (see page 82)

Yui Miles – Drunken Noodles (Pad Kee Mao) from Thailand (see page 106)

Zaleha Olpin – Chicken Rendang from Malaysia (see page 116)

MY FRIENDS AND FAMILY

Thank you to my dearest friend, **Ritu Tandan**, who has been my rock throughout this entire process. We had so much fun exploring, taking photographs, and, of course, eating our way through Old Delhi. The rickshaw rides, the long walk for the famous 'Chinese samosa', and our adventures inside the spice market will always be etched into my memory. Those moments were truly unforgettable! Ritu, I am so grateful for all the brainstorming sessions, for your help testing the recipes, for calming me down when I was anxious, and for taking care of me during my lowest moments. Your unwavering support and friendship over the last 40 years means the world to me.

I have no words to fully express my gratitude to the four people who are my pillars, holding me up and keeping me going every day. **My mother, Shamoli**, who has also written the beautiful foreword for this book, is my greatest inspiration – Mamu, you are my life.

My sister, Madhulika, the wise one – you always have my best interests at heart and are always there to watch my back.

My husband, Tomas, thank you for allowing me to be radikal and for wholeheartedly supporting all my adventures.

And finally, to my nephew, **Yaamir Badhe**, thank you for being a constant source of joy and encouragement in my life. Thank you for your incredible masterclass in history, particularly on the Hellenistic period and Buddhist trails. I am so grateful for the in-depth information you have provided about the historical trade routes, which enriched the culinary history of this book. Your meticulously drawn maps were invaluable and helped me visualise the connections between different cultures and their cuisines. Your expertise and dedication have truly made a difference in bringing this project to life.

MY JOURNEY

Hello, I'm Radhika, and welcome to my culinary world!

As a home cook, recipe developer, and flavour enthusiast with a background in nutrition and dietetics, my love for food and cooking has been shaped by a lifetime of rich experiences. From my early days in the vibrant city of Kolkata to my childhood in the historic city of Gwalior, and later to the dynamic cultural hub of New Delhi, my culinary journey has been one of exploration and discovery. Since moving to the UK, I've continued to blend these diverse influences into my cooking, and this cookbook reflects the flavours and stories that have inspired me along the way.

Growing up in Gwalior, I had the unique privilege of living on the campus of Scindia Kanya Vidyalaya, a renowned girls' school where my mother taught. The school, founded by the illustrious Scindia family, was nestled in a part of the palace grounds – a green oasis teeming with peacocks and fruit orchards. My childhood was filled with the simple joys of climbing mulberry trees, plucking guavas straight from the branches, and savouring the tangy thrill of raw mangoes, or 'kairi', with my younger sister. These experiences instilled in me a deep appreciation for fresh, natural flavours and the vibrant bounty of nature.

My heritage has played a significant role in shaping my culinary journey and fuelling my quest for flavours. With roots in Punjabi, Bengali, and South Indian traditions, I grew up in a home where the kitchen was a melting pot of spices and diverse tastes. My mother's cooking was traditional yet radical, a daily adventure where no two meals were ever the same, and each of her dishes were a delightful exploration of India's regional cuisines. Watching her cook was like witnessing a master conductor orchestrate a symphony, with each spice a note that contributed to the harmonious melody of a perfectly balanced dish. She never relied on recipes or cookbooks – her creativity and innovation in the kitchen were boundless; a trait she has passed down to me and which became the foundation of my own culinary exploration.

My love for food began in childhood, not just as an eater but as an eager observer of the magic that happened in the kitchen. I spent countless hours by my mother's side, absorbing the art of cooking while we chatted about school, friends, and life. This was where I first learned the basics of cooking: not from a textbook, but from the heart – a heart that knew how to blend spices with instinct and passion.

Another profound influence on my culinary journey was my maternal grandmother, Varda, who was an exceptional cook and a culinary expert far ahead of her time. I spent many memorable times with her, watching as she meticulously made pickles and explained the art of balancing flavours. These food memories are etched in my mind and have greatly influenced the way I approach cooking today, always mindful of balance and harmony in every dish.

The influence of my extended family further expanded my culinary horizons. With five maternal aunts (masis) married into different cultural backgrounds – Kashmiri, Tamilian, Hyderabadi Muslim, Sikh, and Punjabi – and with Armenian and Italian family members, our family gatherings

1973-1974 RAMAN
1974-1975 RENU BHALLA
1975-1976 NANDITA SINGH
1978-1979 PREETI ANAND
1979-1980 RADHIKA SETH
1980-1981 NOOPUR VIJAYA
1981-1982 SEEMA THIRANI
1982-1983 APARNA MATHUR
1983-1984 MADHULIKA SETH
1984-1985 SHALINI GUPTA / GARIMA
1985-1986 TANUSHREE SHAH
1986-1987

@GBFOODFESTIVAL

THE
GREAT BRITISH
FOOD FESTIVAL

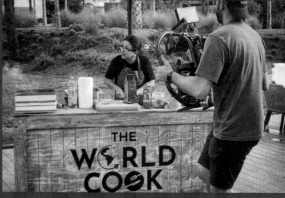

THE
WORLD
COOK

were like a United Nations council of flavours. These experiences enriched my understanding of global cuisines and the beautiful ways in which food can connect people across cultures. My culinary adventures continue today with my Spanish-German husband and his family, adding even more layers of flavour to my journey.

To deepen my understanding of food, I pursued a degree in Food and Nutrition at the prestigious Lady Irwin College in New Delhi, followed by a master's diploma in Dietetics and Public Health Nutrition. My internship at the All-India Institute of Medical Sciences further honed my skills and knowledge, grounding my culinary passion in a strong foundation of nutritional science.

Arriving in the United Kingdom in 1998, I found myself instantly immersed in London's vibrant and diverse culinary scene. The city's melting pot of cultures offered an exhilarating array of cuisines, flavours, and ingredients that ignited my passion for exploring new gastronomic horizons. I discovered Middle Eastern cuisine and fell in love with the flavours. This is when spices and herbs like sumac, za'atar, tahini, and baharat entered my pantry.

London was also the gateway to Europe, where I had the chance to travel to various places on the continent and learn about Mediterranean cuisines. My introduction to Spanish cooking came through my mother-in-law, and I learned many traditional and home-cooked dishes from her, including Catalan fideuà, romesco sauce, and crema Catalana.

My first encounter with Peruvian food was through Martin Morales' ceviche restaurant, one of the first to bring authentic Peruvian cuisine to London. It captivated me so much that I went on to take cooking classes to learn more about the rich flavours and culinary traditions of Peru.

My biggest influences in more recent times have been Yotam Ottolenghi and Sami Tamimi. They have opened another dimension of food, flavours, and culinary realisations that've deepened my appreciation for the art of cooking.

I started Radikal Kitchen seven years ago as a content creator on Instagram, driven by my love for food, cooking, eating, and feeding others. Radikal Kitchen has been inspired by my diverse cultural heritage, passion for flavours, and adventurous palate. This led me to work with brands, developing recipes, creating content, and curating culinary events. My dancing and cooking videos on Instagram drew attention and landed me on TV. In 2022, I represented India in a global TV cooking competition called The World Cook on Amazon Prime. In 2024, I became a finalist on the Channel 4 show Double the Money, hosted by Sue Perkins.

I continue to create content, run cooking classes, develop recipes, and perform chef demos at food festivals. I am also a dedicated member of the Guild of Food Writers and the Chef's Forum.

Through this – my debut book – my culinary journey continues. After all, "It's not the destination, but the journey that matters". I hope you're ready to start yours!

ABOUT THE BOOK

From an early age, I realised that flavours have no boundaries; they seamlessly travel across the world, adapting and integrating into new homes while creating beautiful culinary stories along the way. Having lived in Britain for 30 years, I've been shaped by its vibrant, dynamic, and culturally diverse society, and I now consider myself a global citizen. Living here has only intensified my passion for exploring world cuisines and discovering global flavours.

Flavours Without Borders was born from a desire to capture the unique experience of living in the UK, combined with my love for diverse cuisines. It aims to share stories and recipes that reflect our collective history and showcase the idea that, despite our varied backgrounds, we are all part of a larger, interconnected family.

I continue to be inspired by cuisines from all over the world, and while I don't consider myself an expert, I am an enthusiastic student, eager to learn and explore. In this book, I've made a sincere effort to authentically represent recipes from other cultures, inviting friends to contribute recipes and share their expertise along the way. My goal is to celebrate the diversity of global cuisines and share my journey of discovery with you.

Over the book's largest recipe chapter, I have taken one ingredient and explored its use across three different cuisines, illustrating how historic connections have influenced the evolution of these dishes. Each trio of recipes reflects a journey shaped by significant events and cultural exchanges, such as the ancient Silk Route, the spread of Buddhism across Southeast Asia, and immigration. This remarkable culinary osmosis has allowed flavours to travel, interact, and merge, forging new and unexpected combinations across borders. By examining how a single ingredient transforms in different cultural contexts, we can discover the fascinating ways in which global connections have influenced our food, reflecting a shared heritage that spans continents and traditions.

The final section of the book includes eleven of my 'Radikal Recipes'. These are my own creations where I've put a twist on classic dishes or fused elements from different cultures. I have always loved exploring new flavours and pushing culinary boundaries, and these recipes reflect my fun and adventurous approach to cooking. I hope you have as much fun making these recipes as I did creating them!

And, finally, I hope this book ignites your curiosity and encourages you to experiment with flavours and cuisines you haven't tried before. Whether you decide to experiment in your kitchen or take a virtual journey through history, I want you to feel inspired to cross culinary borders and discover a rich tapestry of global flavours.

This book is an extension of my journey, filled with recipes inspired by the vibrant cultures and flavours that have left an indelible mark on my palate. Each dish is a testament to the power of food in connecting people, breaking barriers, and uniting us through shared gastronomic experiences. Join me as we embark on this culinary odyssey, and let's celebrate a limitless world of flavour together!

THE HISTORY THAT SHAPED THE WORLD'S CUISINES

This section provides an overview of the historical trade routes and conquests which have influenced the world's diverse culinary landscape.

THE SILK ROAD

The Silk Road was an extensive network of trade routes that connected the East and the West, stretching from China to the Roman Empire. Established around the 2nd century BCE, these routes thrived for over 1,500 years. Often regarded as the first global trade route in history, the Silk Road had far greater significance than just the exchange of goods.

The terms 'Silk Road' and 'Silk Route' are often used interchangeably to describe this ancient network that facilitated not only the trade of goods but also the exchange of ideas across continents. The term 'Silk Route' is sometimes used to emphasise the multiple branches, detours, and alternative pathways that made up this intricate web of connections.

Named for the lucrative silk trade, the Silk Road also facilitated the trade of spices, grains, fruits and vegetables, tea, ivory, cotton, wool, precious metals, and much more. The route's significance declined in 1453 when the Ottoman Empire imposed trade restrictions, but its impact on commerce, culture, and history continues to be felt to this day.

One of the most famous travellers of the Silk Road was Marco Polo (1254–1324 CE). Born into a family of wealthy merchants in Venice, Italy, Marco travelled with his father to China when he was just 17 years old.

THE SPICE ROUTE

The Spice Route was a vast network of maritime trade routes that facilitated the exchange of spices and other goods between the East and the West, covering regions from Southeast Asia to Europe. This trade route was crucial for global commerce from ancient times through to the 19th century, driven by the demand for spices like cinnamon, pepper, nutmeg, and cloves, which were prized for their culinary, medicinal, and religious uses.

Initially dominated by Arab traders who connected spice-producing regions with the Middle East and Europe, the route later saw significant involvement from European explorers, particularly Vasco da Gama, whose voyage to India in 1498 marked a turning point in the spice trade. These European explorations, beginning in the late 15th century, marked a turning point in the spice trade, leading to increased European control and the establishment of colonial empires in spice-rich regions. The Spice Route was more than just a trade network; it was a conduit for cultural exchange that spread ideas, religions, and technologies across continents.

Key countries on the route were the Malabar Coast (India), Sri Lanka, Indonesia's Moluccas Islands, and China. It is also important to note the broader regions involved, such as East Africa (including Zanzibar), the Arabian Peninsula (Oman and Yemen), and Southeast Asian regions beyond the Moluccas, like Sumatra and Java. Egypt and the Middle East served as significant intermediaries for the spice trade, facilitating the flow of goods and cultural exchange.

THE MARITIME SILK ROAD

The term 'Maritime Silk Road' refers to the network of sea routes that connected Asia, Africa, and Europe. It was part of the broader Silk Road network, which included both overland and maritime routes.

The Maritime Silk Road encompassed the Spice Route, but it had a broader scope that went beyond just spices. It facilitated the trade of a wide variety of goods, including silk, porcelain, tea, precious metals, and other luxury items, and was a major conduit for cultural, technological, and religious exchanges among civilisations along its paths.

While the Spice Route emerged prominently during the 15th to 17th centuries, driven by European exploration and the quest for direct access to spices, the Maritime Silk Road developed earlier, dating back to ancient times, and played a vital role in cultural and religious exchanges.

PORTUGUESE SETTLEMENTS

Portuguese colonisation began in the early 15th century and continued into the 20th century, establishing a vast maritime empire across Africa, Asia, and South America. Portugal's exploration efforts led to the colonisation of Brazil in 1500, which became the crown jewel of the Portuguese Empire, serving as a major source of sugar, coffee, and later gold and diamonds. In Asia, Portugal established colonies in India, such as Goa, Daman, Diu, and other trading posts like Macau in China and Malacca in Malaysia. Portuguese colonisation was marked by the spread of Christianity, the establishment of the transatlantic slave trade, and the cultural exchange that left lasting impacts on the language, religion, and customs in its former colonies.

FRENCH SETTLEMENTS

French colonisation began in the early 16th century and continued into the mid-20th century, during which France established a vast empire spanning several continents. In North America, France controlled territories such as New France (now parts of Canada and the United States) and established colonies in the Caribbean, including Haiti and Martinique. In Africa, French colonies included Algeria, Senegal, and Madagascar, while in Asia, France colonised parts of India, including Pondicherry, and established French Indochina, comprising modern-day Vietnam, Laos, and Cambodia.

THE BUDDHIST TRAIL IN SOUTHEAST ASIA

The Buddhist trail in Southeast Asia began with the spread of Buddhism from India around the 3rd century BCE, primarily through the efforts of King Ashoka, who sent missionaries to various parts of Asia. Buddhism first took root in Sri Lanka and then spread to mainland Southeast Asia, reaching present-day Myanmar, Thailand, Laos, and Cambodia. This spread was facilitated by trade routes, cultural exchanges, and the adoption of Buddhism by local rulers. Over time, Buddhism deeply influenced the region's culture, art, and architecture, and the spread of its non-violent ethos can be seen in the subsequent popularisation of vegetarian cuisine.

THE MOORISH RULE IN SPAIN

From the 8th to the 15th century, the Moors, a term used by Europeans to describe Muslim people from North Africa and the Iberian Peninsula, dominated large parts of present-day Spain and Portugal. This era began with the Umayyad conquest of Hispania in 711 AD, which led to the establishment of the state of Al-Andalus. The period of Moorish rule in Spain was marked by significant cultural exchange and development, with the introduction of advanced agricultural techniques, distinctive architectural styles, and the flourishing of scholarship and science. However, religious and political conflicts between Muslim Moors and Christian kingdoms sparked the Reconquista, a centuries-long campaign to reclaim the territory. Moorish rule persisted until 1492, when the last Moorish stronghold, the Emirate of Granada, fell to Christian forces, marking the end of Muslim dominion in Spain. Today, the legacy of Moorish culture is still evident in Spain's language, architecture, and cuisine.

THE HELLENISTIC PERIOD

The Hellenistic period, which began with the death of Alexander the Great in 323 BCE and lasted until the emergence of the Roman Empire in 31 BCE, refers to the era when Greek culture, language, and influence spread widely across the Mediterranean, the Middle East, and into parts of Asia. The word 'Hellenistic' derives from the Ancient Greek word 'Hellene', meaning 'Greek'.

Alexander's empire extended from Greece and Egypt in the west to the Indus River Valley in the east, encompassing present-day Afghanistan, Pakistan, and parts of India. This period saw the blending of Greek culture with local customs, leading to significant advancements in science, philosophy, art, and trade. In regions like Egypt and India, Hellenistic influence contributed to the development of new hybrid cultures, such as Greco-Buddhism in India, which merged Greek artistic styles with Buddhist themes.

AUBERGINE
THE AUBERGINE ODYSSEY
IRAN, CHINA, AND INDIA

The journey of aubergines, also known as eggplants, begins in India. From India, the humble aubergine embarked on a remarkable journey across continents, facilitated by the intricate web of trade routes known as the Silk Road. The Silk Road was more than just a conduit for silk; it was a network that connected East and West, facilitating the exchange of goods, ideas, and culture. Aubergines were one of the many agricultural products that travelled these routes, gradually becoming a staple in various local cuisines across Asia and the Mediterranean.

It is believed that aubergines were first introduced to Persia (modern-day Iran) during the Sassanid Empire (224-651 CE) through trade with India. Linguistic evidence supports this theory, as the Persian word for aubergine, 'bademjan', is derived from the Sanskrit word 'vatigagama'. Furthermore, the Hindi word for aubergine, 'baingan', shares this linguistic heritage, illustrating the deep-rooted connections between these regions. Over time, aubergines became a significant ingredient in Persian cuisine in delicious recipes like **Persian Mirza Ghasemi**.

The journey of the aubergine did not stop in Persia; it continued to travel along the Silk Road, eventually reaching China. Aubergines are now widely used in Chinese cuisine, particularly in Sichuan cuisine, which is renowned for its bold flavours and innovative use of ingredients. Their use of aubergines is no exception, and they are often cooked in a variety of ways, including stir fried (as in my **Stir fried Chinese Aubergine**), braised, and roasted, showcasing their versatility and importance in Chinese culinary traditions.

In India, the love for aubergines is evident in its inclusion in countless regional dishes. Each part of the subcontinent has its own unique way of preparing aubergine, highlighting its adaptability and the rich culinary traditions of the region. In North India, Baingan Bharta is a popular dish where aubergines are roasted, mashed, and cooked with tomatoes, onions, and spices. In the West, Vangi Bhaat, from Maharashtra, blends aubergines with spiced rice. The South offers Ennai Kathirikai, a tangy and spicy stuffed aubergine curry from Tamil Nadu, while the East enjoys Begun Bhaja, a simple yet delicious Bengali dish of fried aubergine slices. I'm sharing one of my personal favourites: **Achari Baingan**.

Explore these fantastic aubergine dishes and discover the wonderful fusion of this versatile vegetable and the flavours of Persian, Indian, and Chinese cuisine.

MIRZA GHASEMI AUBERGINE DIP

Iran

Prep time: 20 minutes | Cooking time: 1 hour | Serves 4

Mirza Ghasemi is a traditional Persian dish that originated in the Gilan province of Iran, located along the Caspian Sea. It is a delicious, smoky dip named after Mohammad Qasim Khan, the governor of Rasht during the reign of Nasser al-Din Shah in the 19th century.

Aubergines are popular in Persian cuisine and are frequently used in dips and stews because of their ability to absorb rich flavours.

Mirza Ghasemi is typically served with flatbreads like lavash or pitta. It can be enjoyed as an appetiser, a side dish, or a main course, depending on the context of the meal. I learned this recipe from my talented Persian friend Alireza.

2 large aubergines

3 large ripe tomatoes

4 tbsp vegetable or olive oil

6 cloves of garlic, finely chopped

1 tsp turmeric

1 tsp tomato purée

Pinch of salt and pepper, to taste

4 eggs

Handful of parsley or coriander, chopped,
to garnish

Preheat the oven to 200°c. Pierce the aubergines all over with a fork then place on a baking tray and roast for about 30 to 40 minutes, turning occasionally, until the skin is charred. At the 10- or 20-minute mark, add the tomatoes and roast for 20 to 25 minutes. Alternatively, you can roast both or either directly over a gas flame, or grill them for a smokier flavour.

Once roasted, let the aubergines cool slightly before peeling off the charred skin, then mash the flesh with a fork. Likewise, remove the tomato skin, allow to cool, and grate the tomato flesh.

Heat the oil in a frying pan over a medium heat. Add the chopped garlic and sauté for 1 minute. Add the turmeric and stir for a few seconds. Add the grated tomatoes and tomato purée then cook for a further 5 minutes. Add salt and pepper to taste.

Add the mashed aubergines and continue to cook for 8 to 10 minutes, stirring occasionally.

Make four small wells in the aubergine mixture and crack an egg into each well. Stir gently to combine the eggs with the sauce. Cook until the eggs are fully set and incorporated, about 5 to 7 minutes.

Garnish with fresh herbs and serve hot with a warm flatbread (like lavash or pita) or rice.

STIR FRIED AUBERGINES WITH SESAME AND GARLIC

China

Prep time: 15 minutes | Cooking time: 25 minutes | Serves 4

In Chinese culture, aubergines are valued for their ability to absorb flavours, making them a popular ingredient across the country. The first world cuisine I tasted as a child was Chinese. It was a big culture shock when I discovered how different the Chinese food I'd had in India was from the Chinese food in the UK. Each region of China offers unique flavours and cooking techniques, from the spice of Sichuan dishes to the more delicate flavours of Cantonese cuisine. This journey has deepened my appreciation of China's rich, diverse culinary traditions, and it continues to inspire my cooking. This quick and delicious recipe is perfect for busy weeknights.

5 tbsp vegetable oil

1 medium onion, chopped

1 thumb of ginger, grated

6 cloves of garlic, chopped

2 red chillies, chopped

2 large aubergines, cut into bite-sized chunks

8 tbsp water

2 tbsp dark soy sauce

2 tbsp rice vinegar

1 tbsp rice wine

1 tsp cornflour

3-4 spring onions, chopped

1 tsp sesame oil

2 tbsp toasted sesame seeds

Heat the oil in a wok and add the onions, ginger and garlic and fry for 2 minutes on a medium to high heat. Add the chillies and aubergines and fry for 3 to 4 minutes. Add the water and turn down to a simmer for 10 minutes.

In a separate bowl, combine the soy sauce, rice vinegar, rice wine and cornflour and add it to the aubergines. Continue cooking over a medium-high heat until the liquid reduces by half, then add the spring onions and red chillies.

Drizzle with sesame oil and sprinkle with the toasted seeds before serving.

ACHARI BAINGAN (AUBERGINES COOKED WITH PICKLING SPICES)

India

Prep time: 30 minutes | Cooking time: 40 minutes | Serves 4

Achari Baingan is a North Indian dish that features aubergines cooked in an "achari" gravy. The term "achari" refers to the use of pickling spices and flavours in the preparation of the dish, giving it a distinct and tangy taste reminiscent of Indian pickles (achar).

I made this dish in the first round of Amazon Prime's The World Cook. I was complimented by the famous food critic Jay Rayner, who said the flavours were "bang on." This dish can be a side to a main meal, or it can be the star of the show.

FOR THE AUBERGINE

2 large aubergines, cut into cubes

1 tsp salt

Neutral oil, to deep fry (sunflower or vegetable oil)

FOR THE GRAVY

3 tbsp oil

1 tsp black mustard seeds

1 tsp fenugreek seeds

1 tsp fennel seeds

1 tsp cumin seeds

3-4 green cardamom pods

1 tsp nigella seeds

1 large onion, finely chopped

1 tbsp ginger paste

1 tbsp garlic paste

4 tbsp tomato purée

½ tin of chopped tomatoes, blended (200g)

6 tbsp water, to cook, if required

1 tsp turmeric

1 tsp ground coriander

1 tsp red chilli powder

Salt, to taste

Coriander, chopped, to garnish

FOR THE AUBERGINE

Add 1 teaspoon of salt to the aubergine cubes, mix well, and set aside for 15 to 20 minutes. Rinse the salted aubergine in a colander under cold running water then transfer to a clean kitchen towel. Pat the cubes dry to remove excess moisture. Heat enough oil in a wok to deep fry and fry the aubergine cubes until golden brown, around 12 to 15 minutes. Put the fried aubergines on some kitchen roll to absorb the excess oil and set aside.

FOR THE GRAVY

Heat the oil in a non-stick pan and, when the oil is hot, add the mustard seeds, fenugreek seeds, fennel seeds, cumin seeds, green cardamom pods, and nigella seeds until they start to pop and crackle.

Add the chopped onions and fry on a medium heat for about 12 to 15 minutes until they turn golden brown. Add the ginger and garlic pastes and cook for a further 3 to 4 minutes. Add a few drops of water if you find the mixture is sticking to the base of the pan.

Add the tomato purée, tinned tomatoes, and 3 tablespoons of water to make a thick sauce. Mix well and simmer for 5 minutes on a medium heat. Add the turmeric, ground coriander and chilli powder, then mix well. Add 2 tablespoons of water, then cover and cook for 3 to 4 minutes.

Add the fried aubergine pieces to the spice mix then add salt and mix. Add a little water, cover, and cook the aubergines on low heat for 6 to 8 minutes until soft.

Garnish with chopped coriander leaves and serve.

NOTE

This dish can be made a day ahead and tends to taste even better as the flavours have been given time to develop and meld.

RED KIDNEY BEANS

A BEAN BONANZA

INDIA, SOUTH AFRICA, AND KENYA

From **Rajma** to **Bunny Chow** to **Maharagwe**, the following recipes demonstrate how red kidney beans form a culinary link connecting India, South Africa, and Kenya in delicious harmony!

It is fascinating to see how the historical connections between these countries have influenced and shaped their cuisines over time. Indian migration to South Africa and Kenya during the colonial period brought Indian labourers, traders, and vendors who subsequently introduced their spices, culinary traditions, and cooking methods to the continent, resulting in an evolution of fusion dishes and flavour.

Indian immigration to Durban, South Africa, took place in the 1860s when British colonial authorities brought indentured labourers from India to work in the sugar cane plantations in Natal, the province where Durban was located at that time. The evolution of some regional dishes provides an excellent example of this culinary osmosis, where Indian spices and recipes were integrated into local cuisine. Bunny Chow is a classic example of this, as the inclusion of curry leaves can be attributed to Indian workers, particularly those from South India, where curry leaves are an essential ingredient in the local cuisine. The use of a hollowed-out loaf of bread to serve the curry, on the other hand, is typically South African. This unique combination of Indian curry and African bread is a beautiful example of how recipes are translated and adapted across cultures.

This parallels the historical link between India and Kenya, whereby many Indians migrated to Kenya as labourers during the 19th and 20th centuries, working on railway construction during British colonial rule. This migration and cultural exchange resulted in a coming together of Indian and East African cuisines and culinary traditions. For example, Maharagwe has similarities with Indian Rajma due to the use of red beans and spices, but the Kenyan dish uses fewer spices and does not include whole spices which would be commonly used in the Indian method. The addition of coconut milk is also very traditional in East African cuisine.

The next recipes are special to me because it is exciting to see how the flavours of my favourite Rajma dish have evolved from the streets of North India to the markets of South Africa and the sun-soaked coast of Kenya. Each dish tells a story of resilience, innovation, and culinary creativity. Join me on this flavourful journey and explore how my favourite dish has reinvented itself by embracing local flavours.

MY MOTHER'S RAJMA (RED KIDNEY BEAN CURRY)

India

Prep time: 10 minutes | Cooking time: 40 minutes (or 50 minutes, plus overnight soaking if using dried kidney beans) | Serves 4

Rajma Chawal is a classic North Indian dish featuring red kidney bean curry served with steamed rice. This iconic meal is a staple in many North Indian households, known for its rich flavours and comforting appeal.

'Rajma' is derived from the Hindi word for kidney beans and 'chawal' is the Hindi word for rice. The kidney beans are cooked in a gravy of onions, ginger, garlic, and tomatoes infused with spices. It is creamy, rich, aromatic, and delicious.

For many people, including me, Rajma Chawal is associated with memories of childhood, home-cooked meals, and family gatherings. It's often passed down through generations as a special family recipe - one that holds great sentimental value.

Rajma Chawal holds a special place in my heart as it reminds me of happy mealtimes with my mother and sister. It remains one of my all-time favourites to this day. This recipe is my mother's, and every nostalgic bite brings a sense of culinary delight that I treasure dearly.

200g dried red kidney beans soaked overnight and drained, or 2 x 400g tins of red kidney beans

1.25L water, to cook the dried red kidney beans (if using)

4 tbsp vegetable oil, for cooking

1-2 bay leaves

4-5 green cardamom pods

1 large onion, finely chopped or grated

1 tbsp ginger paste

1 tbsp garlic paste

1 x 400g tin of chopped tomatoes, blended

1 tsp turmeric

1 tsp ground cumin

1 tsp ground coriander

2-3 green chillies (optional)

1 tsp garam masala

1 tsp kasoori methi (dried fenugreek leaves)

A handful of fresh coriander leaves, chopped, to garnish

If using dried kidney beans, add a pinch of salt to the soaked beans then cover with water and cook in a pressure cooker for 10 to 12 minutes. Once tender, remove the beans and set aside. Reserve the cooking water for the sauce.

To make the masala, heat the oil in a pan and add the bay leaves, green cardamom pods and chopped onions. Cook on a medium heat for 6 to 8 minutes until the onions have browned.

Next, add the ginger and garlic paste. Mix well and cook for further 3 minutes, stirring throughout to avoid the mixture sticking to the bottom of the pan.

Add the tomatoes and cook for a further 3 to 4 minutes on a medium heat. Then, add the turmeric, cumin, coriander, and green chillies. Add 2 to 3 tablespoons of water to the masala mix and stir.

If using dried kidney beans, add the pre-boiled beans to the masala and sauté for 3 to 4 minutes. Add the reserved water as required to meet the desired consistency, then mix well and simmer on a low heat for 4 to 5 minutes.

If using the tinned kidney beans, add them to the masala (including the liquid) and sauté for 3 to 4 minutes. Add 500ml of water and simmer for a further 5 minutes.

Check for seasoning then add the garam masala. Crush the kasoori methi in your hands before adding it, then let the sauce simmer for 10 minutes.

Finish with coriander leaves and serve with steaming hot plain rice.

BUNNY CHOW
South Africa

Prep time: 10 minutes | Cooking time: 25 minutes | Serves 4-6

Originating in Durban, South Africa, Bunny Chow consists of a hollowed-out loaf of bread filled with curry. The bread serves as both a container and a way to soak up all the delicious curry sauce, making it a satisfying and filling meal.

The origins of Bunny Chow are closely tied to the history of Indian migration to South Africa and the unique culinary fusion that emerged as a result. The origin of the name 'Bunny Chow' is often speculated. One theory suggests it comes from the Tamil word 'bani' or 'bunny', meaning bread, reflecting the use of bread as a curry container by Indian immigrants. Another attributes the name to a restaurant owner named Banias, who allegedly created the dish and named it 'Banias' Chow' before it was colloquially shortened to 'Bunny Chow'. Others speculate that 'bunny' derives from 'bun and chicken', referring to the bread being filled with chicken curry. Regardless of its origin, Bunny Chow has become a much-loved iconic dish.

This vegetarian version uses kidney beans and aromatic spices, including curry leaves. If you're seeking a delicious meat-free option that embodies the essence of South African cuisine, my kidney bean Bunny Chow is sure to delight your palate!

5-6 tbsp vegetable oil

12-15 fresh curry leaves

2-3 bay leaves

1-inch cinnamon stick

2 dried red chillies

2 medium onions, finely chopped

1 tsp ginger paste

1 tsp garlic paste

1 x 400g tin of chopped tomatoes, blended

½ tsp turmeric

1 tsp medium curry powder

Salt, to taste

2 x 400g tins of red kidney beans

100ml water

1 tsp garam masala

1 small lemon, juiced

A handful of fresh coriander leaves, chopped, to garnish

4-6 large crusty bread buns (approximately one per person)

Heat the oil in a large pan and toss in the curry leaves, bay leaves, cinnamon, and dried red chillies. After 10 seconds, add the chopped onion. Turn the heat to medium and sauté the onions for 4 to 5 minutes until golden-brown.

Add the ginger and garlic pastes, mix well, then cover with a lid. Cook on a medium heat for 5 minutes, stirring regularly to make sure it doesn't stick to the base of the pan.

Tip in the tomatoes and cook for 6 to 8 minutes, again stirring intermittently.

Add the turmeric, curry powder and salt, then add 2 tablespoons of water to make a thick paste.

Add the kidney beans along with the liquid from the cans, then top up with 100ml of water.

Stir well, then bring to the boil and simmer for about 10 minutes or until the sauce has thickened. The gravy should be a thick consistency, or else it will soak too quickly into the bread and become soggy.

Sprinkle in the garam masala, add the lemon juice, and garnish with chopped coriander leaves.

TO SERVE

Slice across the top of each bread bun to create a lid. Then, hollow out the centre of the bun by removing the soft bread inside, leaving a sturdy bread bowl.

Spoon the hot curry into the hollowed-out bread bowl until full, then place the lid on top. Serve with a side salad. Bunny Chow is typically eaten by tearing off pieces of the bread and dipping them into the curry.

KENYAN MAHARAGWE (COCONUT KIDNEY BEANS)

Kenya

Prep time: 10 minutes | Cooking time: 35 minutes (or 1 hour and 30 minutes, plus overnight soaking if using dried kidney beans) | Serves 4

This popular dish from Kenya is made with red kidney beans cooked in a flavourful coconut-based sauce. It's commonly served with rice or ugali, a traditional Kenyan cornmeal porridge.

Maharagwe is the Swahili word for kidney beans. Swahili is widely spoken in East Africa, including Kenya, and many culinary terms and dishes in Kenya have Swahili names due to the influence of Swahili culture and language in the region.

Maharagwe has various regional and personal variations; some recipes include additional vegetables or are sweetened with sugar. The core ingredients of maharagwe are kidney beans, onions, coconut milk, and tomatoes, and when simmered together they create a rich and delicious stew.

Enjoy this flavourful maharagwe stew with your choice of rice, bread, or flatbread. Simply ladle the maharagwe over your preferred accompaniment and savour each bite of this classic Kenyan dish. Bon appétit!

200g dried red kidney beans, soaked overnight and drained, or 2 x 400g tins of red kidney beans, drained

2 tbsp vegetable oil

1 large onion, finely chopped

1 tsp garlic paste

1 tsp ginger paste

1 x 400g tin of chopped tomatoes

1 tbsp tomato purée

½ tsp turmeric

1 tsp ground cumin

1 tsp ground coriander

Salt and pepper, to taste

1 x 400ml tin of coconut milk

A handful of fresh coriander leaves, chopped, to garnish

If using dried kidney beans, rinse and drain the soaked kidney beans. Then, in a large pot, cover the kidney beans with water and bring to the boil. Reduce the heat, cover, and simmer for about 45 to 60 minutes, or until the beans are tender. Drain and set aside.

Heat the vegetable oil in a large saucepan over a medium heat. Add the chopped onion and sauté until translucent, about 5 to 6 minutes.

Stir in the garlic and ginger and cook for another 3 to 4 minutes.

Add the tinned tomatoes and tomato purée to the saucepan and mix well. Cook for 5 to 7 minutes on a medium heat. Add 2 tablespoons of water if you find the mixture is sticking to the bottom of the pan.

Stir in the dried spices, salt, and pepper. Mix well to combine.

Pour in the coconut milk and stir to combine, then add extra water according to the desired consistency. Bring the mixture to a simmer and let it cook for 5 to 10 minutes.

Add the cooked kidney beans, or tins of kidney beans, to the saucepan and stir gently to coat the beans with the creamy sauce.

Simmer for an additional 5 to 10 minutes to heat through and thicken the sauce.

Garnish with fresh coriander and serve the hot maharagwe with cooked rice, bread, or flatbread.

RICE

RICE ROUTES

IRAN, AZERBAIJAN, AND INDIA

As a staple ingredient in the cuisines of India, Persia (modern-day Iran), and Azerbaijan, rice has played a central role in the culinary traditions of these regions for centuries. The Silk Road, an ancient network of trade routes, served as a conduit for cultural exchange, allowing for the diffusion of cooking techniques, spices, and recipes across vast territories. This interconnectedness has left an indelible mark on the evolution of rice dishes in these regions.

In Persian cuisine, rice is not merely a side dish: it is a central component of many meals. The Persian method of cooking rice, known as polo or pilaf, involves cooking rice with a variety of ingredients like meat, vegetables, nuts, and spices. A key element that sets Persian rice dishes apart is the generous use of saffron, which not only gives a rich golden hue to the rice but also enhances the dish's aroma and flavour.

Pulao, a one-pot dish of rice cooked in seasoned broth with various meats, vegetables, and spices, travelled along the Silk Road from Persia to Central Asia and India. Azerbaijan, located at the crossroads of Eastern Europe and Western Asia, was heavily influenced by Persian culinary traditions and adapted the Persian polo into its own variation known as plov, characterised by fragrant saffron, dried fruits, nuts, and often lamb or chicken.

Pulao's arrival in India is also linked to these interactions. The Mughal emperors, with their Central Asian and Persian heritage, were patrons of the arts and gastronomy, leading to the fusion of Persian, Central Asian, and Indian culinary traditions. This fusion resulted in dishes like pulao and biryani being incorporated into Indian cuisine. In India, pulao has taken on various regional forms, such as the mild and fragrant Kashmiri pulao, the spicy and vibrant Hyderabadi pulao, and the sweet and aromatic Lucknow pulao.

Biryani is a culinary masterpiece that epitomises the synthesis of Persian and Indian cuisines. Originating from the Persian polo, biryani was transformed by the Mughal emperors who brought Persian chefs and cooking techniques to India. This dish incorporates Indian spices such as cumin, coriander, and cardamom, and employs a sophisticated layering technique of marinated meat and partially cooked rice. The marination process and the use of saffron and dried fruits reflects age-old Persian influences, and the modern biryani stands as a testament to the rich cultural and culinary exchange between Persia and India.

These rice recipes - **Zereshk Polo ba Morgh**, **Sirin Plov** and **Tehri** – capture the essence of this grain's culinary journey, reflecting its rich heritage and evolution across India, Persia, and Azerbaijan.

ZERESHK POLO BA MORGH

Iran

Prep time: 15 minutes, plus 15 minutes to brew the saffron | Cooking time: 1 hour 15 minutes | Serves 6-8

"As a kid, this sweet and sour dish was always at the centre of most family gatherings and special occasions, but despite this, it's actually a very easy dish to cook and perfect for a midweek dinner. The combination of rice mixed with saffron, caramelised onions and tangy barberries really make this dish unique, super tasty and aromatic. Over the years, this dish has gained popularity around the world and can be found on the menu at many Persian restaurants." - Alireza Sarrafan, @alirez.foods

I want to say a massive thank you to my good friend Alireza for sharing this exquisite recipe. An expert in Persian cooking, he hosts his own cooking show on Persian TV. I had the opportunity to collaborate with him on his show, exploring and discussing Indian street food. Besides our love of good food, we've been brought together by the commonalities in our cuisines. In the future, we hope to host dining events in London to showcase that exact culinary osmosis, so watch the space!

FOR THE BREWED SAFFRON

¾ tsp saffron threads, ground then brewed in 8 tbsp boiling water for 15 minutes (makes 8 tbsp)

FOR THE CHICKEN

3 tbsp sunflower oil

6-8 skinless chicken legs or breast

1 large white onion, chopped

1 clove of garlic, chopped

1 tsp turmeric

Salt and pepper, to taste

2 tbsp tomato purée

4 tbsp cream (single or double)

2-4 tbsp brewed saffron

1 tbsp butter, to serve

FOR THE ZERESHK POLO

400g white basmati rice, washed and soaked in salted water for 30 minutes

2 green cardamom pods

150g dried barberries (zereshk), washed

2 tbsp rose water

1 large white onion, sliced into half moons

2 tbsp sunflower oil

3 tbsp butter

1 tbsp sugar (optional)

4 tbsp brewed saffron

Salt and pepper, to taste

FOR THE CHICKEN

Add the oil, chicken, onions, garlic, turmeric, salt and pepper to a pan and fry for 7 to 8 minutes until golden-brown, making sure to turn the chicken often so it's evenly cooked.

Stir the tomato purée in 250ml of water, then add this to the chicken and let it cook, covered, on a low-medium heat for 45 to 55 minutes (depending on the size of the chicken cuts). Halfway through cooking, add the cream and 2 to 4 tablespoons of brewed saffron. While the chicken is cooking, prepare the rice.

FOR THE ZERESHK POLO

Bring a litre of water to the boil with a dash of salt and oil, then add the soaked rice. Reduce the heat to medium and cook for 8 to 9 minutes until the rice is al dente. Drain the rice through a strainer and rinse with cold water to halt the cooking process.

Spread the rice in the base of a large pot, place the cardamom pods on top of the rice, then cover the lid with a tea towel and steam for 30 to 40 minutes on a very low heat until fluffy and aromatic.

While the rice cooks, re-hydrate the berries by soaking them in water with 1 tablespoon of rose water. Ensure the berries are fully covered and let them soak for 15 minutes. Fry the sliced onion in 2 to 3 tablespoons of oil and set aside.

In a separate pan, melt some butter on a low heat, then add the re-hydrated barberries, sugar, fried onion, and 2 tablespoons of brewed saffron, and cook for about 4 minutes. Immediately remove from the heat to avoid burning the berries.

Once the rice is cooked, scoop 10 to 12 tablespoons of the cooked rice into a bowl, add another 2 tablespoons of brewed saffron and 4 tablespoons of cooked barberries, then gently mix them together and set aside.

TO SERVE

Just before serving, stir a tablespoon of butter through the chicken and allow it to melt into the sauce.

Spread a bed of the white, fluffy rice over a large plate, then layer it with the saffron and barberry rice before topping it with the remaining barberries and onions. Serve with crispy rice from the bottom of the pot (known as 'tahdig') and the aromatic chicken.

SHIRIN PLOV (SWEET RICE PILAF)

Azerbaijan

Prep time: 25 minutes, plus 20 minutes soaking the rice | Cooking time: 35 minutes | Serves 4

Shirin Plov is a traditional Azerbaijani dish that is often served at weddings, festivals, and other special occasions. It is a sweet and aromatic rice dish made with saffron, dried fruits, and nuts, giving it a rich and flavourful taste.

Plov, also known as pilaf or pulao, is a traditional one-pot rice dish originating from Central Asia and is common in other countries on the Silk Route. It is typically made by cooking rice in a seasoned broth, along with meat, vegetables, and a blend of spices. I have made a vegetarian version of this sweet plov, incorporating a delightful blend of spices and vegetables for a wholesome and warming dish.

300g basmati rice

3 tbsp vegetable oil

1 onion, finely chopped

2-inch piece of ginger, finely diced

2 tsp ground coriander

1 tsp turmeric

½ tsp ground cumin

½ tsp ground cinnamon

½ tsp ground cardamom

2 carrots, shredded

30g dried apricots, chopped

30g raisins

500ml water

Salt and pepper, to taste

30g flaked almonds, to garnish

30g pistachios, chopped, to garnish

30g walnut, chopped, to garnish

30g candied citrus peel, to garnish (optional)

Rinse the rice and soak in cold water for 20 minutes. Meanwhile, heat the oil in a large cooking pot and sauté the chopped onion for 5 minutes until softened. Add the diced ginger and ground spices and cook for another minute until fragrant.

Add the shredded carrots, chopped apricots, and raisins to the pot and cook for 2 to 3 minutes, stirring occasionally. Add the rinsed rice and stir well to coat with the spices and vegetables. Pour in the water and bring to the boil.

Reduce to a simmer, then cover and cook for 15 to 20 minutes, or until the rice is cooked through and the liquid has been absorbed. Remove from the heat and let the rice sit, covered, for 5 minutes.

Fluff the rice with a fork and season with salt and pepper to taste. Transfer to a serving platter and garnish with the chopped nuts and candied citrus peel (if using). Serve warm and enjoy!

TEHRI (VEGETABLE PULAO)

India

Prep time: 15 minutes, plus 20 minutes soaking the rice | Cooking time: 30 minutes (or 20 minutes if using a pressure cooker) | Serves 4

Tehri is a simple and easy-to-prepare one-pot meal from the state of Uttar Pradesh in India. It's made with rice and vegetables like potatoes, peas, carrots, and cauliflower. This wholesome and nutritious dish is usually enjoyed with yoghurt and pickles.

Tehri holds a special place in my heart and evokes cherished memories of my mother. She would often make this dish, especially when she was working long hours and wanted to give us a quick, nourishing meal. The warmth and love she put into preparing tehri made it more than just food; it was a comforting hug on a plate, and a testament to her care and dedication. She affectionately called it "ghee-bhath" (rice and ghee), and its aroma and flavours bring back the comfort of home.

250g basmati rice

3 tbsp ghee or vegetable oil

2 bay leaves

1 tsp cumin seeds

1-inch cinnamon stick

1 black cardamom pod

3 cloves

6 black peppercorns

2 medium onions, finely sliced

1 tsp turmeric

1 tsp chilli powder

1 tsp ground coriander

Salt, to taste

200g cauliflower, cut into florets

100g peas

1 potato, peeled and cubed

500ml water

Fresh coriander leaves, to garnish

Rinse the rice then soak for 15 to 20 minutes in cold water. Drain and set aside.

In a pressure cooker or pot, heat the ghee or oil, then add the bay leaves, cumin seeds, cinnamon stick, cardamom, cloves, and peppercorns. After 30 seconds, add the sliced onion and sauté for 6 to 7 minutes on a medium heat until the onions turn golden-brown.

Add the turmeric, chilli powder, ground coriander, and salt, then cook for 1 minute before adding the rice and mixing well.

Add the chopped vegetables, mix, then add the water and pressure cook for 10 to 12 minutes or until the rice is tender (timing can vary depending on your cooker). Cover and simmer for 20 to 25 minutes if using a standard pot.

Garnish with coriander leaves and serve hot with yoghurt dip, salad, pickles and pappad (papadams).

FLOUR

FLATBREAD TALES ALONG THE SILK ROAD
INDIA, TURKEY, AND AFGHANISTAN

As we traverse the historic Silk Road, we discover a delightful thread that connects the cuisines of India, Turkey, and Afghanistan: the versatile and beloved flatbread. These humble yet delicious creations not only showcase the culinary ingenuity of each region but also symbolise the blending of cultures along an ancient trade network. The Indian **Paratha**, Turkish **Gözleme**, and Afghan **Bolani** each bring unique flavours and textures, reflecting the distinct ingredients, cooking techniques, and cultural influences that have shaped them. Their evolution on the Silk Road is a fascinating tale of adaptation and innovation, as these flatbreads travelled across borders and evolved to suit local tastes and traditions.

The origins of these flatbreads are deeply intertwined with the history of the Silk Road. This vast network of trade routes facilitated not only the exchange of goods but also the sharing of culinary practices and ingredients. As traders and travellers moved from Central Asia to the Indian subcontinent and beyond, they carried with them recipes and techniques that would evolve in new environments. The common feature in all three flatbreads is the way they are prepared. Indian paratha, Turkish gözleme, and Afghan bolani are all made using rolled dough that is stuffed with a variety of fillings before being cooked.

Parathas, a staple in Indian cuisine, are typically made from wholewheat flour. The dough is layered with ghee or oil and can be stuffed with a variety of fillings such as spiced potatoes, paneer, or lentils. The dough is then folded and rolled again to create a flaky texture before being pan fried to golden perfection.

Gözleme, a traditional Turkish flatbread, is similar in its preparation. The thin, unleavened dough is filled with ingredients like spinach, feta, potatoes, or ground meat.

Similarly, Afghan bolani is a stuffed flatbread, commonly filled with potatoes, spinach, lentils, or pumpkin. The dough for bolani is like that of paratha and gözleme, showcasing the shared techniques across these regions.

Beyond their culinary uses, these flatbreads hold significant cultural value in their respective regions. In India, paratha is a common part of everyday meals and festive occasions, symbolising home-cooked comfort and hospitality. Gözleme, deeply rooted in Turkish village traditions, is now enjoyed widely across the country, including urban areas, and symbolises the country's rich culinary heritage. Bolani, a beloved Afghan snack, is often made for special occasions and represents the warming flavours of home-cooked food.

These flatbreads are the perfect vehicle for dips and chutneys – in true 'radikal' spirit, try mixing and matching them with other recipes, like Coriander Kiwi Chutney (see page 198), Beetroot Raita (see page 170) and Aloo Chukauni (see page 172).

PANEER PARATHA (FLATBREAD STUFFED WITH PANEER)

India

Prep time: 15 minutes, plus 20 minutes resting | Cooking time: 30 minutes | Makes 6-7

Parathas are a popular Indian flatbread made from wholewheat flour, water, and ghee (clarified butter). Parathas can be enjoyed plain or stuffed with various fillings, like potatoes, peas, or onions. Paneer paratha is a type of stuffed paratha filled with grated paneer (cottage cheese). The filling is seasoned with spices like cumin, coriander, and chilli powder before being added to the dough.

Parathas hold a special place in the hearts of many, evoking warm memories of winter brunches and cosy meals. There's something so magical about biting into a hot, flaky paratha, and these stuffed parathas are a real treat during the colder months, bringing joy and comfort with every bite. In Old Delhi, there is a charming street called Paranthe Wali Gali, where one shop boasts over 70 varieties of stuffed parathas. It is a paradise for paratha lovers and a testament to the endless creativity and enduring popularity of this delightful dish.

FOR THE DOUGH

240g wholewheat flour

½ tsp salt

1 tbsp vegetable oil

100-120ml water (adjust as needed)

FOR THE FILLING

150g paneer, grated

1 small onion, finely chopped

1-2 green chillies, finely chopped

1 tsp fresh ginger, grated

½ tsp ground cumin

1 tsp garam masala

½ tsp chaat masala or mango powder

2 tbsp fresh coriander leaves, finely chopped

Salt, to taste

3-4 tbsp ghee or oil, for frying (or as needed)

To prepare the dough, combine the wholewheat flour, salt, and oil in a large mixing bowl. Gradually add the water, stirring continuously, and knead the mixture into a smooth, soft dough (be careful to add the water bit by bit so the dough doesn't become too sticky). Cover the dough with a damp cloth and let it rest for 15 to 20 minutes.

To make the filling, combine the grated paneer, chopped onion, green chillies, grated ginger, ground cumin, garam masala, chaat masala, chopped coriander leaves, and salt in a bowl. Mix well to evenly distribute the spices and ingredients.

Divide the dough into six to seven equal portions and shape them into balls. Roll each ball out on a floured surface into a small circle. Place a golf ball-sized portion of the paneer filling in the centre of each circle, then carefully bring the edges of the dough together to seal the filling inside. Shape it back into a ball, then gently roll out into a paratha (about 6 to 7 inches in diameter), being careful not to let the filling spill out.

To cook the parathas, heat a tawa or skillet over a medium heat, then place the rolled-out paratha on the hot tawa and cook for about 2 minutes. Flip it over and brush with ghee or oil before flipping again - once or twice - until both sides are cooked. It should take about 4 minutes per paratha. Serve warm with raita and pickle.

GÖZLEME

Turkey

Prep time: 40 minutes, including 30 minutes resting | Cooking time: 20 minutes | Makes 6-8

Gözleme is a traditional Turkish flatbread made from thinly rolled dough. It is traditionally filled with ingredients like spinach, feta cheese, minced meat, potatoes, and herbs, before being cooked on a griddle. Part of the flatbread family associated with the Silk Route, gözleme shares similarities with other flatbreads found along this historic trade route, reflecting the rich, interconnected food traditions of Central Asia, the Middle East, and beyond.

Gözleme can be eaten as both a main course and a snack. It is typically served hot and can be enjoyed on its own or with accompaniments such as yoghurt, salad, or a squeeze of lemon.

This vegetarian version of gözleme with spinach and feta is a family favourite. The shape of gözleme can vary slightly depending on the region and its cooking style, but it is usually a flat, round, semicircular, or oval shape that is easy to eat with your hands.

FOR THE DOUGH

240g plain flour

½ tsp salt

2 tbsp olive oil

175ml water (adjust as needed)

FOR THE FILLING

100g fresh spinach, finely chopped

100g feta cheese

1 small onion, finely chopped

½ tsp freshly ground black pepper

1 tbsp olive oil

Salt, to taste

To prepare the dough, first combine the flour and salt in a large mixing bowl. Add the oil and gradually add the warm water, mixing continuously until a soft dough forms. Knead the dough on a floured surface for about 5 minutes until smooth and elastic, then cover the dough and let it rest for at least 30 minutes. Meanwhile, combine the filling ingredients and set aside.

Divide the dough into equal portions, then roll each piece into a thin circle or oval on a floured surface. Place the filling on one half of the dough, leaving a small border around the edge. Fold the dough over to enclose the filling and press the edges to seal. Use some water or oil to seal, if necessary.

Heat a griddle over medium heat and lightly grease with oil. Cook the gözleme for 2 to 3 minutes on each side until golden-brown and crisp. Brush with a little more olive oil, if desired, and serve warm.

BOLANI
(STUFFED FLATBREAD)
Afghanistan

Prep time: 40 minutes, including 20 minutes' rest | Cooking time: 30 minutes | Serves 4

Bolani is a stuffed flatbread from Afghanistan, sort of like a vegetable-filled calzone. It is made with a thin, unleavened dough filled with ingredients like spinach, leeks, lentils, or potatoes. The dough is folded over the filling, sealed, and then pan fried or baked in an oven until golden-brown and crispy. Bolani can also be made in different shapes, like triangles or circles, depending on the region and cooking style.

Bolani is often served with a yoghurt dip or chutney as an appetiser, snack, or side dish.

FOR THE DOUGH

240g plain flour

½ tsp salt

2 tbsp vegetable oil, plus more for frying

175ml warm water (adjust as needed)

FOR THE FILLING

2 large leeks, cleaned and finely chopped

4 spring onions, finely chopped

2 tbsp fresh coriander leaves, chopped

1 tsp ground cumin

1 tsp ground coriander

½ tsp red chilli flakes (optional)

Salt and pepper, to taste

To prepare the dough, first combine the flour and salt in a large mixing bowl. Add the oil and gradually add the warm water, mixing continuously until a soft dough forms. Knead the dough on a floured surface for about 5 minutes until smooth and elastic, then cover with a damp cloth and rest for at least 20 minutes. Meanwhile, combine all the filling ingredients and set aside.

Divide the dough into four to six equal portions. Roll each portion into a ball, then roll each ball out on a floured surface into a thin circle. Place a generous spoonful of the filling on one half of the dough circle, then fold the dough over the filling to form a semi-circle. Press the edges to seal or use a fork to crimp and seal the edges.

Heat 2 tablespoons of vegetable oil in a large skillet over a medium heat, then fry each bolani for about 2 to 3 minutes on each side, or until golden-brown and crispy. Add more oil as needed to fry the remaining bolani. Serve warm with a side of yoghurt or chutney for dipping.

SAMOSA

A SAVOURY TRAVELLER ON THE SILK ROAD
UZBEKISTAN, INDIA, AND TANZANIA

Samosas are enjoyed worldwide, coming in various shapes, sizes, and names. This has always sparked my curiosity – whose samosa is it anyway, and why so many variations?

The samosa's journey on the Silk Road is believed to have started in Central Asia, and the origin of the word itself can be traced back to Persian literature, where this triangular-shaped snack was known as 'sanbosag', possibly translating to 'lovely triangles', and later evolving into the Central Asian 'samsa'. The **Uzbek Samsa** is a popular savoury pastry from Uzbekistan with significant influences from Persian cuisine; it is typically stuffed with onions, meat and various spices, and baked in a tandoor oven, imparting a unique flavour to the pastry.

From there, the samosa spread along the trade routes, reaching India by the 13th or 14th century. In India, it underwent significant transformation to adapt to local tastes, incorporating spices such as pepper, ginger, and coriander, and often replacing meat with vegetables like potatoes and peas, which were introduced to India by the Portuguese.

In India, the classic samosa is typically filled with a mixture of spiced potatoes, peas, onions, ginger, and green chillies, enjoyed nationwide from roadside stalls to high-end restaurants. This versatile snack boasts a variety of regional variations, each reflecting local tastes. The **Punjabi Samosa** features a thicker, flakier crust and a hearty filling of spiced potatoes, peas, and sometimes paneer. Bengali Shingara incorporates potatoes, cauliflower, and peanuts, and is known for its thinner, more delicate crust. Hyderabad's Keema Samosa offers a non-vegetarian twist with minced meat, usually mutton or chicken, cooked with aromatic spices and herbs. In South India, samosas are often smaller with a thinner crust, and fillings range from the classic potato mixture to unique options like lentils, onions, or even sweet versions with coconut and jaggery.

The journey of the samosa continued along the Silk Road through the Middle East, and eventually to the coastal regions of East Africa to the tropical shores of Zanzibar, an archipelago off the coast of Tanzania, where it has become a beloved snack infused with local flavours. Tanzania was not directly on the traditional Silk Road, which primarily connected China with the Mediterranean, but it was part of the broader network of trade routes often referred to as the Maritime Silk Road. The Maritime Silk Road was a crucial component of the ancient Silk Road, facilitating the exchange of goods, culture, and ideas between the East and the West through sea routes.

Zanzibar's rich history as a trading hub has resulted in a fusion of African, Arab, and Indian influences, which can be tasted in the unique filling of Zanzibari samosas. These samosas – as shown in my **Tanzanian Sambusa** – often feature a combination of local spices, seafood, and other regional ingredients, reflecting the island's diverse culinary heritage.

SAMSA

Uzbekistan

Prep time: 25 minutes, plus 30 minutes resting | Cooking time: 1 hour | Makes 10-12

Uzbek Samsas are savoury triangular pastries that are popular in Uzbek cuisine and other Central Asian countries. Similar in shape to an Indian samosa, it features a thicker, bread-like crust. Like in an Indian samosa, the filling for samsas can vary, but it is usually made with spiced minced meat (beef, lamb, or chicken) and onions. Some variations also include pumpkin, potatoes, or other vegetables. The exterior has a satisfying crunch, while the interior layers absorb the flavourful meat juices, creating a delightful contrast of crispy and moist in every bite.

I have made this with chicken mince and deep fried it, though they can also be baked in the oven, if you prefer.

FOR THE DOUGH	*FOR THE FILLING*
240g plain flour	*1 tbsp vegetable oil*
½ tsp salt	*1 medium onion, finely chopped*
3 tbsp olive oil or melted butter	*250g chicken mince*
175ml water (adjust as needed)	*1 tsp ground cumin*
1 tbsp ghee, melted	*1 tsp ground coriander*
Neutral oil, to deep fry	*½ tsp black pepper*
	1 tsp paprika
	Salt, to taste

To make the dough, combine the flour and salt, then add the oil or melted butter and mix well. Gradually add the water and knead until you get a smooth, elastic dough. Cover the dough with a damp cloth and rest for 30 minutes.

To make the filling, heat the oil in a pan over medium heat. Add the onion and sauté for 5 minutes until translucent. Add the chicken mince and cook for 12 to 15 minutes before adding the ground spices and salt. Cook for another 5 minutes until the spices are well combined and the chicken is cooked through, then remove from the heat and allow to cool.

Once the dough has rested, sprinkle a work surface with a little flour and roll the dough into a thin rectangular sheet, approximately 7 to 8 inches in length. Cover the sheet with melted ghee then, starting at one edge, roll the dough tightly like a cigar. Cut this into equal pieces to make about ten to 12 dough balls.

Roll each dough ball out into a thin circle, about 6 to 7 inches in diameter, using a rolling pin. Cut each circle in half, then divide the filling evenly between each semi-circle. Bring the opposite sides of the dough together to make a triangle, then pinch the corners and edges together to seal the filling and shape the triangle.

Once all the samsas have been formed, heat plenty of oil in a deep pan and fry until golden-brown and crispy on both sides, about 6 to 7 minutes.

PUNJABI SAMOSA

India

Prep time: 25 minutes, plus 30 minutes resting | Cooking time: 40 minutes | Makes 12

Samosas are the most popular snack across India, with many regional variations reflecting the local cuisines. The Punjabi samosa from northern India features a spicy potato filling, which is a classic. As you move south to Andhra Pradesh, the filling changes to a tangy mix of tamarind and peanuts. In West Bengal, samosas are known as singharas, and they're often filled with a cauliflower-based mixture. The variations are endless, highlighting the rich and diverse culinary traditions across India. Punjabi samosas are so delicious, and I have fond memories of enjoying them in Bengali Market in Delhi – a place well-known for its street food shops during my college days.

FOR THE DOUGH

250g plain flour

½ tsp carom seeds

½ tsp salt

4 tbsp ghee or olive oil

60ml water (adjust as needed)

Neutral oil, to deep fry

FOR THE FILLING

1 tbsp vegetable oil

1 tsp cumin seeds

1 tsp coriander seeds, crushed

1 tsp fennel seeds

1 tsp ginger, grated

2 green chillies, finely chopped

100g green peas

4 medium potatoes, boiled and mashed

½ tsp turmeric

1 tsp garam masala

1 tsp dried mango powder (amchur),
or 1 tbsp lemon juice

Salt, to taste

Fresh coriander leaves, chopped

To make the dough, combine the flour, carom seeds, and salt. Add the ghee or oil and mix well with your fingers until the mixture resembles breadcrumbs. Gradually add the water and knead to form a firm, smooth dough. Cover the dough with a damp cloth and set aside for at least 30 minutes to rest.

To make the filling, heat the vegetable oil in a pan over a medium heat. Add the cumin seeds, crushed coriander seeds, and fennel seeds and sauté for 1 minute. Add the grated ginger and green chillies and sauté for another minute.

Add the green peas and cook for 4 to 5 minutes until tender, then add the mashed potatoes, turmeric, garam masala, amchur (or lemon juice), and salt. Mix well and cook for 5 minutes, then add the coriander leaves. Remove from the heat and set aside to cool.

Divide the dough into six equal balls then roll each ball into a circle (about 6 to 7 inches in diameter). Cut the rolled-out dough into two semi-circles, then take one half and form a cone by folding it and sealing the edge with water. Fill the cone with 2 to 3 tablespoons of the potato filling, then seal the top edge of the cone with water and press firmly to ensure it's well sealed.

Heat some oil in a large pan and deep fry the samosas until golden-brown and crispy, about 6 to 7 minutes. Serve with mint and/or tamarind chutney.

SAMBUSA

Tanzania

Prep time: 20 minutes, plus 30 minutes resting | Cooking time: 1 hour | Makes 8-10

Sambusa is a popular snack and street food in Zanzibar, Tanzania. While the traditional filling often includes spiced potatoes, peas, or minced meat, fish sambusas are also common, particularly in coastal regions where seafood is in abundance. In Zanzibar, fish sambusas are typically made with a filling of finely chopped or flaked fish, seasoned with spices and herbs.
This recipe includes a tuna filling, inspired by the Spanish empanada.

FOR THE DOUGH

240g plain flour

½ tsp salt

2 tbsp olive oil or butter, melted

250ml water (adjust as needed)

Neutral oil, to deep fry

FOR THE FILLING

2 tbsp olive oil

1 small onion, finely chopped

3 cloves of garlic, minced

2 tbsp tomato purée

1 tsp ground coriander

½ tsp turmeric

½ tsp black pepper

Salt, to taste

1 x 200g tin of tuna

1 lemon, juiced

2 tbsp fresh parsley, chopped

To make the dough, combine the flour and salt in a bowl, then add the oil or melted butter and mix well. Gradually add water and knead to form a smooth, elastic dough, then cover with a damp cloth and allow to rest for 30 minutes.

To make the filling, heat the olive oil in a pan and sauté the onion and garlic for 5 minutes on a medium heat. Add the tomato purée, thin with 1 tablespoon of water, and cook for 3 to 4 minutes. Add the spices and salt, mix well, then add the tinned tuna and cook for 5 minutes on a low heat. Remove from heat and stir in the lemon juice and parsley, then set aside to cool.

Divide the dough into eight to ten equal portions and roll each portion into a ball. Roll out each ball into a thin circle on a floured surface (about 6 to 7 inches in diameter), then cut each circle in half to form two semi-circles. Take one semi-circle and form it into a cone shape. Seal the edge with a little water, then fill the cone with 2 tablespoons of the tuna filling.

Seal the top of the cone by pressing the edges together with water, then repeat with the remaining dough and filling. Bring some neutral oil, like vegetable or sunflower, to a high heat, then deep fry the sambusas in hot oil until golden and crispy, about 5 to 7 minutes. Serve with chutney, mayonnaise, or your dip of choice.

NOTE

Feel free to add peas or chopped olives to this recipe to create your own unique mix.

TOFU

FAITH AND FOOD
CHINA, JAPAN, AND INDIA

In this chapter, we explore how the spread of Buddhism has shaped the cuisines of India, China, and Japan. As we trace the journey of this ancient religion from its birthplace in India, along the Silk Road to China, and eventually to Japan, we will uncover how Buddhist philosophy has left a distinct impression on the culinary practices and recipes of these regions.

Buddhism played a significant role in the popularity of vegetarianism, and thus the use of tofu in China and Japan. Buddhist monks, prohibited from consuming meat, inspired the development of many vegetarian dishes and meat substitutes such as tofu and seitan. Tofu, a soy-based product, was already present in China before the arrival of Buddhism, but it became more popular with the spread of Buddhism due to its role as a protein-rich substitute for meat. Today, tofu is a central part of Chinese cuisine, featuring in numerous traditional and contemporary dishes, from Sichuan **Mapo Tofu** to the sweet tofu puddings of southern China.

Buddhism's influence on Japanese cuisine was equally profound. As in China, Buddhism popularised vegetarianism in Japan, leading to the creation of shojin-ryori, a type of vegetarian cuisine still practiced in some Buddhist temples today. Shojin-ryori emphasises simplicity, balance, and mindfulness in food preparation and consumption, mirroring Buddhist principles. **Dengaku Tofu**, with its simple yet flavourful preparation, became a favoured dish in Buddhist temple cuisine.

Another aspect of this history is the birth of Indo-Chinese cuisine in India. It all began in the late 18th and early 19th centuries when Hakka-speaking Chinese immigrants settled in Kolkata (formerly Calcutta), the capital of British India at the time. These Chinese immigrants, who were mostly silk traders, dentists, carpenters, and leather tannery owners, started adapting their cooking techniques to the local ingredients available in India. The result was a unique fusion of Indian and Chinese flavours, which became known as Indo-Chinese cuisine. The dishes were an Indian interpretation of Chinese food, combining the deep fried, spicy flavours Indians love with Chinese ingredients like soy sauce and vinegar. Some of the most popular dishes in Indo-Chinese cuisine include **Paneer Manchurian** (a deep fried dish also made with chicken, cauliflower, prawns, fish, or mutton), Sichuan or "Schezwan" Sauce (a spicy sauce made with dried red chillies), and Mixed Chow Mein Noodles. As tofu is not a traditional part of Indian cuisine, I have chosen a paneer recipe to demonstrate the fusion of Indo-Chinese flavours. Paneer is very popular in India, especially among Hindus who, like Buddhists, promote non-violence (ahimsa) and are therefore often vegetarian. Paneer, an Indian cottage cheese, serves as a meat-free protein source akin to tofu and is thus a more accurate regional example of the influence of vegetarianism.

MAPO TOFU

China

Prep time: 10 minutes | Cooking time: 25 minutes | Serves 4

Mapo Tofu is a delightful, mouth-tingling dish that perfectly balances the vibrant flavours of Sichuan cuisine. It is known for its spicy, bold flavours and features a combination of tofu (bean curd) and minced meat (usually pork or beef) cooked in a spicy and savoury sauce.

The vegetarian version of Mapo Tofu replaces the meat with mushrooms but keeps the signature spicy and numbing addition of the Sichuan peppercorns and chilli bean paste.

The 'Mapo' in Mapo Tofu is in honour of the creator of the dish. 'Mapo' translates to 'pockmarked old woman' in English, where 'Ma' means 'pockmarked' and 'Po' means 'old woman' or 'grandmother'. The name refers to a woman who ran a small restaurant in Sichuan province and gave the world this iconic dish.

Mapo tofu is usually served hot and enjoyed with steamed rice.

4 tbsp vegetable oil

400g firm tofu, cubed

1 tsp Sichuan peppercorns, bruised in a pestle and mortar

250g chestnut mushrooms, chopped

1 medium onion, diced

2 tbsp ginger, grated

2 tbsp garlic, finely chopped

1 tsp Chinese five spice

2 tbsp Shaoxing rice wine

3 tbsp doubanjiang (spicy fermented bean paste)

1 tbsp soy sauce

1 tsp chilli oil

250ml vegetable stock

1 tsp sesame oil

¼ tsp sugar

3-4 spring onions, chopped, to garnish

Heat 2 tablespoons of vegetable oil in a wok or large pan over a high heat, then add the tofu cubes and pan fry until golden on all sides. Remove and set aside.

In the same wok or pan, lower the heat and gently toast the bruised Sichuan peppercorns for 1 to 2 minutes. Transfer to a bowl and set aside.

Turn to medium-high heat and add the remaining oil. Fry the mushrooms until the liquid has evaporated and the mushrooms become golden and start to lightly crisp. Add the onion, ginger, garlic, and fry for 2 minutes, then add the toasted peppercorns and Chinese five spice and continue to fry for 1 minute.

Add the rice wine, doubanjiang, soy sauce, and chilli oil and mix well. Then, stir in the stock and bring to the boil. Once boiling, turn down to a simmer for 10 minutes until the sauce has reduced and thickened.

Finally, return the fried tofu to the sauce and mix until it is well coated. Allow the tofu to simmer for 3 to 5 minutes before adding the sesame oil, sugar, and spring onions. Serve with hot rice or noodles.

REIKO'S DENGAKU TOFU

Japan

Prep time: 45 minutes | Cooking time: 30 minutes | Serves 4

Dengaku Tofu is a traditional Japanese dish where firm tofu is grilled or broiled and coated with a sweet and savoury miso glaze. The term 'dengaku' refers to a style of cooking where food is skewered and grilled, often featuring a miso-based sauce. This is one of the most traditional and highly appreciated dishes in Japan. By using simple ingredients, you can create a subtle and sophisticated flavour, like a piece of art on a plate.

I want to thank Reiko Hashimoto (@hashicooking) for this delightful Dengaku Tofu recipe. My introduction to Japanese vegetarian cooking was at her class almost 10 years ago. She was one of the first to start Japanese cooking classes in London, and her passion and expertise have inspired many, including myself. Reiko has written several cookbooks that feature a vast selection of recipes that make Japanese cuisine accessible and enjoyable to all. This recipe features three types of dengaku: white, dark, and green.

600g firm tofu

FOR THE WHITE DENGAKU

4 tbsp white miso paste

1 tbsp mirin

1 tbsp sugar

2 tbsp water

2 egg yolks

FOR THE DARK DENGAKU

1 tbsp black sesame seeds, freshly ground

1 tbsp white miso paste

½ tsp water (if necessary)

FOR THE GREEN DENGAKU

1 tbsp white miso paste

2 tsp shiso leaves, freshly ground (or coriander or Thai basil)

Wrap the tofu with kitchen paper and place a heavy weight on top of it to help squeeze out the excess water. Leave to drain for a couple of hours, then slice the tofu in half and set aside.

To make the white dengaku, mix all the ingredients, except for egg yolks, together. Once mixed well, add to a small pan and cook on a low heat, stirring continuously. Cook for about 2 to 3 minutes until the mixture becomes quite sticky, then add the egg yolks and simmer for a further minute, stirring very quickly and mixing well. Remove from the heat and leave to cool.

To make the dark dengaku, simply mix the ground black sesame seeds into the white miso. As the ground sesame is dry, the texture may become too thick – just add a little water to thin it out, if required.

To make the green dengaku, mix the ground shiso into the white miso until it turns green.

Slice the pressed tofu into 12 even pieces. Turn the grill to a medium heat then brush a little oil all over the tofu. Cook for 3 to 4 minutes on both sides. Once grilled, paste the dengaku miso on top of the tofu pieces, making four pieces per colour/dengaku flavour. Put the tofu back under the grill and cook for a further 2 minutes or until the dengaku miso starts to bubble up and char slightly.

PANEER MACHURIAN

India

Prep time: 20 minutes | Cooking time: 25 minutes | Serves 4

Paneer Manchurian is a popular Indo-Chinese dish that features cubes of paneer (Indian cottage cheese) cooked in a spicy, tangy sauce.

Indo-Chinese Manchurian dishes are a popular fusion cuisine that combine Chinese cooking techniques with Indian flavours and ingredients. The origin of this unique culinary tradition can be traced back to the early 20th century when Chinese immigrants, primarily of Hakka descent, settled in Kolkata (formerly Calcutta), India. These immigrants brought with them their traditional cooking methods and recipes, which gradually began to incorporate local Indian spices and ingredients, leading to the creation of Indo-Chinese cuisine.

Manchurian dishes are characterised by their bold flavours and creative combination of ingredients. They typically involve deep frying vegetables or meat then tossing them in a dark red, spicy, sweet, tangy, and umami sauce.

This dish can be eaten as a starter or a main dish and enjoyed with fried rice or noodles.

FOR THE FRIED PANEER

4 tbsp cornflour

4 tbsp plain flour

½ tsp black pepper

¼ tsp salt

125ml water

250g paneer, cut into cubes

Neutral oil, to deep fry

FOR THE SAUCE

3 tbsp vegetable oil

1 tbsp garlic, finely chopped

1 tbsp ginger, finely chopped

2 green chillies, finely chopped (optional)

1 large onion, finely chopped

5-6 spring onions, chopped, plus extra to garnish

1 green pepper, chopped

2 tbsp soy sauce

1 tbsp red chilli sauce (such as srirarcha or Maggi chilli sauce)

2 tbsp tomato ketchup

1 tbsp malt vinegar

Salt and pepper, to taste

Combine the cornflour, plain flour, black pepper, and salt in a mixing bowl. Add the water to make a smooth batter and coat the paneer with the batter.

Heat the neutral oil in a wok or pan over a medium heat, then deep fry the coated paneer cubes until they are golden-brown and crispy. Remove and drain on paper towels.

In a wok or large pan, warm 3 tablespoons of vegetable oil over a medium-high heat and add the chopped garlic, ginger, and green chillies. Sauté for a minute until fragrant. Add the chopped onions and sauté until they turn golden-brown, then add the chopped pepper and sauté for 2 to 3 minutes.

Stir in the soy sauce, chilli sauce, tomato ketchup, and vinegar. Mix well, then season with salt and pepper to taste. Add the fried paneer cubes to the sauce and mix well. Cook for a further 2 to 3 minutes to allow the paneer to absorb the flavours of the sauce.

Garnish with more chopped spring onions and serve hot with rice or noodles or as an appetiser.

NOTE

Paneer is a type of fresh cheese in Indian cuisine. It is a non-melting cheese, similar in texture to firm tofu. This dish, and many other paneer dishes, can also be made with firm tofu to make them vegan.

CURRY POWDER

CURRY POWDER'S TASTY TRAVELS
THE UK, VIETNAM, AND GERMANY

The global love for curry powder can be traced back to the British colonial era when British officers and traders developed a taste for the rich and complex flavours of Indian cuisine. Eager to replicate these flavours back home in Britain, they created curry powder as a convenient spice blend that captured the essence of Indian curries in a simplified form.

It's important to note that the term 'curry' holds a distinct meaning in Indian cuisine compared to its usage in the West. In India, 'curry' refers to a gravy or sauce that serves as the base for various dishes. This sauce can be made from a diverse blend of spices, herbs, and ingredients, resulting in a wide range of flavours and textures. Contrary to Western understanding, the term 'curry' does not refer to a specific dish or a standardised spice blend in India. Instead, it describes a category of dishes featuring rich and flavourful sauces or gravies.

One might be surprised to learn that the ubiquitous 'curry powder' found in Western supermarkets is not a staple in traditional Indian kitchens. While its roots lie in India's spice heritage, Indians prefer a nuanced approach, using a blend of whole and ground spices and distinctive mixes unique to regions, dishes, and family recipes. Nevertheless, the love and use of curry powder spread far and wide, becoming one of the most popular gastronomic exports following Britain's imperial expansion.

Some notable examples of countries that adopted curry powder from the British include Japan, where it was introduced by British traders in the mid-19th century, leading to the creation of Japanese curry. The United Kingdom itself embraced curry powder, incorporating it into the national diet and giving rise to many British-Indian dishes, such as **Coronation Chicken**. In Vietnam, French colonial influence brought curry powder, and its use is evident in dishes like Vietnamese **Cà Ri Chay**. In Germany, curry powder became a popular ingredient, leading to the creation of **Currywurst**, a beloved street food of curry sauce and bratwurst sausage.

The widespread adoption of curry powder is a testament to its versatility and enduring appeal. From its origins in the British colonial era, curry powder has travelled across the globe, influencing and being embraced by various cultures. Its introduction to Japan, Australia, the United Kingdom, South Africa, Vietnam, and Germany demonstrates how this spice blend has been seamlessly integrated into diverse culinary traditions, creating unique dishes in each region.

JANET'S CORONATION CHICKEN

United Kingdom

Prep time: 10 minutes | Cooking time: 20 minutes | Serves 4

Coronation Chicken was created to celebrate the coronation of Queen Elizabeth II in 1953. The recipe was developed by Constance Spry, a renowned florist and cookery writer, and Rosemary Hume, a respected chef and founder of the L'Ecole du Petit Cordon Bleu cookery school in London. This dish, featuring cold chicken in a creamy curry sauce, is typically served with rice and peas. Over time, it has become a beloved classic in British cuisine, and it's often enjoyed as a sandwich filling or salad.

This recipe is from my lovely 88-year-old neighbour, Janet. She shared it with me during a live Instagram cooking session to celebrate the Queen's historic platinum jubilee in 2022.

1 tbsp vegetable oil

1 onion, chopped

2 chicken breasts, diced

Salt and pepper, to taste

3 tbsp mayonnaise

6 tbsp plain Greek yoghurt

1 tbsp curry powder

1 tbsp lemon juice

2 tbsp raisins

2 tbsp dried apricots, chopped

1x 432g tin of pineapple chunks (272g drained weight)

Heat the oil in a pan and sauté the onions for 4 to 5 minutes until translucent. Remove and set aside.

Season the diced chicken with salt and pepper and add to the frying pan. Add a little extra oil, if necessary, then cook for 10 to 12 minutes until the chicken is cooked through. Remove from the pan, shred with two forks if desired, then set aside to cool.

In a large mixing bowl, mix the mayonnaise, Greek yoghurt, curry powder, and lemon juice together until smooth and creamy. Add the shredded or chopped cooked chicken to the bowl and stir well to coat the chicken evenly with the sauce.

Stir in the raisins, apricots, and pineapple chunks, season with salt and pepper, and serve as a salad or in a sandwich.

CÀ RI CHAY

Vietnam

Prep time: 15 minutes | Cooking time: 35 minutes | Serves 4

Cà Ri Chay is a vegetarian Vietnamese coconut-based curry which is typically served as a main course with rice or a baguette to help mop up the flavourful sauce. The dish's rich coconut milk base is enhanced by a Vietnamese-style curry powder, known for its milder flavour compared to Indian or Thai curry blends.

Curry powder has been used in several Vietnamese dishes since the French colonial period in the 19th and early 20th centuries. Many South Indians, particularly Tamils from the French territories of Pondicherry and Karikal, migrated to Vietnam seeking better job prospects and trade opportunities, and brought their spices with them – including curry spice blends. Over time, Vietnamese chefs adapted and incorporated these flavours into their own dishes, creating their own blend of curry powder and unique fusion recipes that blended Indian and Vietnamese flavours.

4 tbsp vegetable oil

1 block of firm tofu, cut into cubes

1 large onion, thinly sliced

2 cloves of garlic, minced

1 thumb of ginger, minced

2 tbsp curry powder

1 tsp turmeric

1 large carrot, sliced

2 medium potatoes, peeled and diced

1 green pepper, chopped

1 x 400ml tin of coconut milk

500ml vegetable stock

1 tbsp soy sauce

2 tbsp fish sauce

1 tbsp sugar

Salt and pepper, to taste

2 tbsp coriander leaves, chopped, for garnish

4 lime wedges, to serve

Heat 2 tablespoons of vegetable oil in a large pan over a medium-high heat. Add the tofu cubes and fry until golden-brown on all sides. Remove from the pan and set aside.

In the same pan, add the remaining vegetable oil and sauté the sliced onion until translucent, then add the minced garlic and ginger and cook for another 3 to 4 minutes. Sprinkle in the curry powder and turmeric and cook for 1 minute to release their flavours.

Add the vegetables, coconut milk and vegetable stock, and stir well to combine. Then, add the soy sauce, fish sauce, sugar, and season with salt and pepper to taste. Bring the mixture to a boil, then reduce to a simmer. Cover and cook for about 20 minutes, or until the vegetables are tender.

Return the fried tofu to the pan and stir to combine. Cook for 5 minutes to heat the tofu through, then garnish with chopped fresh coriander leaves. Serve with lime wedges and rice or crusty bread.

CURRYWURST SAUCE
Germany

Prep time: 5 minutes | Cooking time: 20 minutes | Serves 4

Currywurst consists of a tangy tomato curry sauce atop a sliced sausage (typically bratwurst). It's a popular German street food and is often accompanied by fries.

The sauce in currywurst is called "curry" because it prominently features curry powder, a spice blend that originated from the British adaptation of Indian spice mixes. After World War II, British soldiers stationed in Germany brought curry powder, a product of British colonial history, with them. Herta Heuwer, a Berlin resident, obtained this curry powder from the soldiers and mixed it with ketchup to create the now-famous currywurst sauce.

2 tbsp vegetable oil

1 small onion, finely chopped

1 clove of garlic, minced

250ml tomato ketchup

50ml water

1 tsp apple cider vinegar

1 tbsp light soft brown sugar

1 tbsp Worcestershire sauce

2 tsp curry powder, plus extra for sprinkling

½ tsp paprika

Salt and pepper, to taste

Heat the vegetable oil in a saucepan over medium heat, then add the finely chopped onion and sauté for 5 minutes until it becomes soft and translucent. Add the minced garlic and cook for another 1 to 2 minutes until fragrant.

Stir in the ketchup, water, apple cider vinegar, and brown sugar and mix until combined. Add the Worcestershire sauce, curry powder, and paprika and stir well. Simmer the sauce on a low heat for 10 minutes, stirring occasionally, until thickened slightly. If the sauce is too thick, you can add a bit more water to reach the desired consistency. Season to taste with salt and pepper.

To serve, pour the warm sauce over cooked bratwurst or sausage slices and sprinkle with a little extra curry powder for an authentic touch.

NOTE
Add 2 teaspoons of red chilli sauce to the above if you like a bit of heat!

FISH

SALT, SPICE, AND THE FRUITS OF THE SEA
PORTUGAL, INDIA (GOA), AND BRAZIL

Portuguese colonial influence has left an enduring legacy in the state of Goa (India) and Brazil, weaving a rich tapestry of cultural and culinary connections across continents. From the historic port city of Porto in Portugal to the vibrant streets of Panaji in Goa, India, and the picturesque coastal town of Paraty in Brazil, this journey encapsulates the essence of Portuguese heritage and its global impact.

Salted cod, or 'bacalhau', is a cornerstone of traditional Portuguese cuisine, valued for its versatility and long shelf life, especially during times of exploration and trade. Before being cooked, the fish is typically soaked to remove the excess salt and then used in a variety of dishes, such as **Bacalhau à Brás**. The influence of this Portuguese staple extends to its former colonies, like Bacalhau Guisado and Bolinhos de Bacalhau in Goa, and the popular Bacalhau com Natas in Brazil.

In Goa, Portuguese rule began in the early 16th century and lasted for over 450 years. The influence on the local cuisine is profound and enduring, particularly noted in the use of vinegar, which imparts a distinctive tangy flavour to many dishes. One of the most iconic Goan dishes, vindaloo, derives its name from the Portuguese 'vinha d'alhos', a marinade of wine and garlic, but it's now a spicy, tangy pork curry. Sorpotel, made from pork offal and blood, is inspired by the Portuguese dish Sarrabulho and is known for its rich, spicy, and tangy flavours. **Caldinho**, as shown in this collection, is a mild, coconut-based curry which also highlights the Portuguese influence. Its name originates from 'caldeirada', meaning fish stew, and it borrows Portuguese techniques of simmering fish in a thin broth (as opposed to the region's more traditional thicker curries). The introduction of ingredients like cashews, tomatoes, and potatoes by the Portuguese has also left a lasting impact on Goan cuisine.

The influence of Portuguese colonisation on Brazilian cuisine is extensive, creating a diverse blend of flavours that incorporates Portuguese, African, and native South American elements. Dishes like Feijoada, a rich black bean stew with pork, highlights the legacy of this cultural fusion, with its combination of Portuguese culinary traditions and African ingredients and techniques. It was originally introduced by African slaves who had been brought to work in the cane fields, and over time was adapted with different meats and spices. Similarly, **Moqueca**, a traditional Brazilian seafood stew, showcases the combination of Indigenous, African, and Portuguese influences in Brazilian cooking. The dish is made with fish cooked in a rich broth made from coconut milk, tomatoes, onions, and coriander. It gets its unique flavour and vibrant colour from dendê (palm oil), introduced by African slaves. The Portuguese also added their own touch by bringing in unique cooking methods and adding peppers and onions.

Besides their lasting impact on these cuisines, the Portuguese have significantly influenced the lifestyle, religion, festivities, and fiestas in both Goa and Brazil. In Goa, the Portuguese introduced Christianity, which is now a major religion in the region, and this religious influence is evident in the numerous churches and cathedrals, such as the Basilica of Bom Jesus and Se Cathedral. Festivals like Carnaval and Sao Joao, featuring vibrant parades, music, and dance, reflect the deep-rooted Portuguese cultural heritage. Similarly, in Brazil, the Portuguese influence is seen in the widespread practice of Catholicism, with grand celebrations of religious events like Carnival, which has become one of the most famous festivals in the world.

VITOR'S BACALHAU À BRÁS

Portugal

Prep time: 20 minutes, plus 12 hours to de-salt the cod | Cooking time: 30 minutes | Serves 4

Bacalhau à Brás is a traditional Portuguese dish made with shredded salt cod (bacalhau), onions, and thinly chopped fried potatoes, all bound together with eggs. The dish is typically garnished with black olives and sprinkled with fresh flat leaf parsley.

The dish originated in the Bairro Alto neighbourhood of Lisbon during the second half of the 19th century. 'Brás' is the name of its creator, and the 'à Brás' technique is often used to describe other dishes that use the same method of binding ingredients together with eggs. This is often served as a main course or as part of a larger meal.

Thank you, Vitor, for sharing your mother's recipe with me. It is truly special to have an authentic recipe straight from Lisbon.

400g bacalhau (salted cod)

50ml olive oil

3 medium onions, thinly sliced

6 cloves of garlic, chopped

500g fried potato sticks (shop-bought)

6 large eggs, beaten

Salt and pepper, to taste

3 tbsp parsley, chopped, to garnish

30g black olives, pitted

Rinse the salted cod under cold running water to remove any surface salt, then place in a large bowl or container filled with cold water. Soak the salted cod for around 12 hours or overnight, changing the water one or two times, to remove the excess salt. This process helps to rehydrate the fish and eliminate the excess saltiness, making it suitable for cooking. Once ready, flake the de-salted cod into small pieces and set aside.

Heat the olive oil over a medium heat and sauté the onion for 10 to 12 minutes until it starts to turn golden. Add the garlic and sauté for another minute before tipping in the flaked cod. Stir and cook for another minute.

Add half of the potato sticks and mix well, then pour in the beaten eggs and stir quickly. Remove from heat, season to taste, and allow the eggs to cook in the residual heat from the pan. Add the remaining potato sticks and mix. (All pans are different so, if required, return the eggs to a gentle heat to cook the eggs through.)

Serve immediately, garnished with chopped parsley and black olives.

GOAN FISH CALDINHO

India

Prep time: 15 minutes | Cooking time: 40 minutes | Serves 4

In Goan cuisine, Caldeirada (or Caldinho) de Peixe typically refers to a mild coconut-based fish curry. This dish is an amalgamation of Portuguese and Goan flavours and cooking techniques. The term 'caldinho' means 'little broth' or 'light broth' in Portuguese, reflecting this curry's thinner consistency compared to other Goan curries. This dish blends Portuguese influences, such as the technique of simmering fish, with Goan spices and coconut milk, creating a unique and flavourful fish stew.

This is typically served with steamed rice to soak up the broth's warming spices, and it's enjoyed as a main course with traditional Goan sides of vegetables and pickles.

3-4 tbsp coconut oil

1 white onion, finely sliced

3 cloves of garlic, minced

2 fresh chillies, cut in half

2 large tomatoes, chopped

1 tsp turmeric

½ tsp ground cumin

1½ tsp ground coriander

1 tsp black pepper, freshly ground

1 x 400ml tin of coconut milk

250ml water

1-inch ball of tamarind, soaked in 125ml hot water

500g fish fillet (such as pomfret, kingfish, cod, or tilapia)

Salt, to taste

2 tbsp coriander, chopped, to garnish

Heat the coconut oil in a large pot over medium heat, then add the sliced onions and sauté for 5 minutes until they become translucent. Add the minced garlic and green chillies and cook for another 2 to 3 minutes until fragrant.

Stir in the chopped tomatoes and cook for 8 minutes until they soften and begin to break down. Then, add the turmeric, cumin, coriander, pepper, and cook for another 3 minutes. Add 2 tablespoons of water if you find the mixture is sticking to the pan.

Pour in the coconut milk and water and bring the sauce to a gentle boil. Add the tamarind pulp, then cover and simmer for 5 minutes.

Finally, add the fish and simmer for 15 minutes, or until the fish is cooked through. Season to taste with salt, then serve hot with rice and a sprinkling of chopped coriander.

NOTE

You can also season the fish with turmeric and salt, fry it until golden brown, and then add it to the gravy in the last step for extra flavour.

ADEMAR'S GRANNY'S FISH MOQUECA

Brazil

Prep time: 15 minutes | Cooking time: 35 minutes | Serves 4

Moqueca is a traditional Brazilian fish stew that originated in the states of Bahia and Espírito Santo. This dish is a fusion of Indigenous, African, and Portuguese culinary influences, reflecting the diverse cultural heritage of the region.

The stew typically features a rich and flavourful base made with coconut milk, tomatoes, onions, garlic, and various herbs and spices. One of the key features of Bahian Moqueca is the use of red palm oil (dendê oil), a richly coloured palm oil that gives the stew its distinctive reddish-orange hue.

The dish is often served with rice, farofa (toasted cassava flour), and fresh coriander, and garnished with lime wedges.

I want to thank my friend Ademar for sharing his grandmother's traditional recipe. I am honoured to have the opportunity to learn and recreate such an authentic recipe.

1kg firm white fish fillets (such as cod, halibut, or snapper), cut into chunks.

1 tbsp lime juice

Salt and pepper, to taste

3 tbsp red palm oil or olive oil

1 bay leaf

2 large onions (1 chopped; 1 sliced thickly)

5 cloves of garlic, minced

1 tsp paprika

2 tomatoes, sliced thickly

3 peppers (red, green, and yellow), sliced thickly

1 x 400ml tin of coconut milk

30g fresh coriander, chopped

2 limes, cut into wedges, to serve

1 tsp red chilli flakes

2-3 red chillies, sliced

Season the fish with lime juice, salt, and pepper and set aside.

Heat 2 tablespoon of oil in a large, wide cooking pot. Add the bay leaf, chopped onion and garlic and sauté for 5 minutes, then sprinkle over the paprika and stir.

Arrange the sliced onions, tomatoes, and peppers in layers, one on top of the other, in the pot, then place the fish in layers on top of the vegetables. Pour over the coconut milk, pop the lid on, and cook for 15 to 20 minutes. Check if the fish is cooked, then pour the final tablespoon of red palm oil on top and cover with the lid. Leave to simmer for another 10 minutes.

Garnish with coriander leaves, lime wedges, chilli flakes and sliced chillies before serving hot with rice.

PRAWNS

SPICE TRAILS AND PRAWN TALES

INDIA, SRI LANKA, AND MACAO

In this section, join me on a culinary adventure across the south of Asia. We begin in India with a creamy **Malabar-style Prawn Curry**, then hop across the Palk Strait in the Bay of Bengal to Sri Lanka for some fiery **Devilled Prawns**. Finally, we set sail to Macau to savour the boldness, spice, and zest of **Macanese Garlic Prawns**. These delicious recipes illustrate the fascinating culinary impact of trade and cultural exchange across these countries and their cuisines.

It all began with India's maritime trade routes that connected it with Southeast Asia, including Sri Lanka and the regions that later became Macau and China. The historical trade between India and Sri Lanka, involving Arab and Jewish merchants, led to the exchange of goods and spices in these regions. As a result of the vibrant trade, ports became the hub for the spice trade and attracted traders from across Asia, the Middle East, and Africa.

The culinary connections between Kerala, Sri Lanka and Macau were further enhanced when Portuguese explorer Vasco da Gama established spice trade routes in the 15th century. Following Vasco da Gama's successful voyage, the Portuguese state sent additional expeditions to Kerala and the surrounding regions to expand trade. In Kerala and Sri Lanka, the Portuguese introduced various ingredients like chillies, potatoes, and tapioca, which were incorporated into local dishes.

Chillies played a significant role in creating a culinary connection between Kerala, Sri Lanka, and Macau. After their introduction by Portuguese traders in the late 15th and early 16th centuries, they became an integral part of local cuisines in these countries. The Portuguese also introduced tomatoes and marination techniques that used vinegar and spices, which greatly influenced the cooking of meat and seafood dishes in Kerala.

Macanese cuisine in particular evolved as a vibrant fusion of Portuguese and Asian flavours. The Portuguese first arrived in Macau in the early 16th century, seeking a strategic base for trade with China and markets in East Asia. Macau was formally established as a Portuguese settlement in 1557, resulting in the development of a unique blend of Chinese and Portuguese culinary influences.

In the recipes that follow, the spices and flavours of each of these regions meet and marry in a global culinary affair! I chose these recipes not only because they are delicious, but also because they showcase a variety of textures, from a creamy curry to a sizzling stir fry. They also highlight the incredible versatility of chilli and other common ingredients and cooking styles across the three cuisines.

MALABAR-STYLE PRAWN CURRY

India

Prep time: 15 minutes | Cooking time: 30 minutes | Serves 4

Malabar-style Prawn Curry is a delightful seafood dish originating from the coastal regions of South India, particularly Kerala. This curry is renowned for its creamy texture and vibrant flavours, crafted with a blend of aromatic spices including mustard and fenugreek seeds, dried chillies, and turmeric. These spices are gently tempered in oil to release their essence before being combined with coconut milk and tangy tamarind.

The star of this dish is the fresh prawns, which are cooked to perfection in the flavourful coconut-based curry. It's traditionally served with steamed rice.

This dish is really special to me because I learned it from my nani (my maternal grandmother) who was from Mangalore and an expert in South Indian regional cuisines. This was also my signature dish on season one of Amazon Prime's The World Cook.

3 tbsp coconut or vegetable oil

2 tsp black mustard seeds

½ tsp fenugreek seeds

10-12 curry leaves

2 onions, finely sliced

2 green chillies, cut in half

6-8 cloves of garlic, crushed

½ tin of chopped tomatoes, blended (200g)

500ml water

1 tsp turmeric

1 tsp ground coriander

Salt, to taste

500g prawns, shelled and deveined

1 x 400ml tin of coconut milk

1 golf ball-sized piece of tamarind, soaked in 125ml water or 2 tbsp malt vinegar

A small handful of fresh coriander leaves, chopped, to garnish

Heat the oil in a heavy bottom saucepan on a medium heat, then add the mustard seeds and let them splutter.

Then, add the fenugreek seeds, half the curry leaves, and the sliced onions. Fry for a minute before adding the green chillies. Continue to fry for 8 to 10 minutes over a medium heat until the onions begin to change colour to a light brown.

Add the garlic and fry for another minute or so before adding the tomatoes and cooking for 6 minutes until softened. Add 125ml of water and continue to cook until the tomatoes turn a deep red. Turn down to a simmer for 2 minutes.

Add the turmeric, coriander, and salt and cook for a further minute, making sure the gravy is not sticking to the bottom of the pan. Add another 125ml of water and stir.

Next, add the prawns and cook over a low heat for 6 to 7 minutes with the lid on, stirring halfway through. Add the remaining water to the gravy.

Add the coconut milk, remaining curry leaves, and bring to the boil.

Turn down to a simmer, then squeeze the tamarind pulp to extract a thick paste and add this to the curry. Simmer for 5 minutes. Garnish with chopped coriander leaves and serve immediately with rice.

ROSHI'S DEVILLED PRAWNS

Sri Lanka

Prep time: 15 minutes, plus 30 minutes marinating | Cooking time: 15 minutes | Serves 4

In Sri Lankan cuisine, a 'devilled' dish refers to a style of preparation where the ingredients, often including meat or seafood, are cooked in a spicy and tangy sauce. The term 'devilled' indicates a fiery and robust flavour profile, characteristic of Sri Lankan cuisine.

Devilled dishes are known for their bold and vibrant flavours, with a balance of heat from the chillies and a tanginess from the vinegar or lime juice. The sauce typically coats the main ingredient, whether prawns, chicken, or fish, and creates a mouthwatering dish that pairs well with rice or bread.

Devilled dishes are deeply rooted in the country's rich culinary heritage. They are a fusion of Chinese and Indian flavours and cooking methods but have a history of European influence. From the 16th to the 18th century, Sri Lanka was occupied by the Portuguese and then the Dutch, and the use of fiery spices (Portugal) and tangy sauces (Netherlands) reflects the influence of these cuisines. This delightful recipe comes from my talented food blogger friend, Roshi (@roshis_food_melodies), who hails from Sri Lanka and is an expert in its cuisine.

500g king prawns, shelled and deveined

½ tsp salt

1 tsp ground black pepper

½ tsp garlic powder (optional)

½ lime, juiced

2 tbsp vegetable oil

6-7 cloves of garlic, finely chopped

1 tsp ginger, finely chopped

2 tsp chilli flakes (according to taste)

1 large onion, cut into small chunks

2 medium green peppers, cut into small chunks.

1 large tomato, cut into chunks

FOR THE SAUCE

1 tbsp light soy sauce

1 tbsp tomato ketchup

1 tbsp oyster sauce

½ tsp cornflour

¼ tsp sugar

3-4 tbsp water

Devein and clean the prawns then marinate them with salt, black pepper, garlic powder (if using) and lime juice for 30 minutes.

Heat the oil in a wok or frying pan and add the garlic and ginger. Fry for a few seconds and then toss in the marinated prawns. Cook for a few minutes on high heat until the prawns turn pink.

Reduce the heat and add the chilli flakes, onions, and green peppers and sauté for 2 minutes.

Add all the ingredients for the sauce along with the tomato chunks. Mix well and continue cooking on a medium heat for 1 minute.

Check for seasoning and serve immediately.

MACANESE GARLIC PRAWNS

Macau

Prep time: 15 minutes | Cooking time: 10-15 minutes | Serves 4

Macanese Garlic Prawns, or Aomen da Suan Xia, is a traditional dish from Macau that highlights the region's unique blend of Chinese and Portuguese influences.

Reflecting the multicultural heritage of Macau, this dish blends Chinese cooking techniques and ingredients with Portuguese flavours and spices. The use of garlic, chillies, and coriander reveals the dish's distinctive Portuguese influence, while the prawns, ginger and soy sauce reflect classic Chinese flavours.

Macanese Garlic Prawns are typically served as a main course alongside steamed rice or noodles. Alternatively, they can be enjoyed with crusty bread to soak up their delicious sauce.

800g large prawns, peeled and deveined

Salt and pepper, to taste

2 tbsp olive oil

2 tbsp butter

10 cloves of garlic, minced

3-4 red chillies, thinly sliced

1 tbsp fresh ginger, grated

2 tbsp soy sauce

1 tbsp oyster sauce

½ lemon, juiced

A handful of coriander leaves, chopped, to garnish

Crusty bread or cooked rice or noodles, to serve

Rinse the prawns under cold water and pat dry before seasoning with salt and pepper.

Heat the olive oil and butter in a large skillet or wok over a medium heat, then add the minced garlic and sliced chillies to the pan. Sauté for about 30 seconds until fragrant.

Add the grated ginger and stir fry for another 30 seconds.

Add the prawns to the pan and stir fry for 2 to 3 minutes until they start to turn pink and are almost cooked through.

Stir in the soy sauce and oyster sauce, then season to taste. Stir well to coat the prawns evenly with the sauce.

Continue cooking for another 2 to 3 minutes, stirring frequently.

Remove the pan from the heat and top with the lemon juice.

Garnish with chopped coriander leaves and serve immediately with crusty bread, rice, or noodles.

MUSSELS

THE FRENCH CONNECTION

FRANCE, INDIA, AND VIETNAM

From the elegant boulevards of Provence to the vibrant city of Pondicherry and the bustling streets of Phan Thiet, the French colonial legacy has intertwined with local traditions, creating a unique tapestry of culture and cuisine that bridges continents and centuries.

The French colonial presence in Pondicherry (now Puducherry) began in 1674 and lasted until 1954. During this period, Pondicherry became a prominent French enclave in India, marked by the distinct French influence on its architecture, culture, and cuisine. The French established grand boulevards, colonial villas, and public buildings, leaving a lasting architectural legacy. French cooking techniques and dining culture were integrated into local practices, with items like wine and cheese became more common. Quiches, too, were made using local spices and vegetables, and fish curries were prepared with a French-style roux along with Indian spices and coconut milk. The French game of boules, often referred to as pétanque, is still played in Pondicherry. This traditional French game has been preserved as part of the cultural heritage of the region.

French colonialism in Vietnam introduced a rich array of French ingredients, cooking techniques, and dishes that have become deeply woven into Vietnamese cuisine. One of the most iconic examples is the Vietnamese bánh mì, a delightful fusion of French baguette stuffed with traditional Vietnamese ingredients like pickled vegetables, coriander, and various meats. This beloved sandwich perfectly embodies the culinary marriage of French and Vietnamese flavours.

But the French influence doesn't stop there. Vietnamese coffee culture, now famous for its strong, sweet iced coffee with condensed milk, has its roots in French colonialism. The French introduced coffee to Vietnam, and the Vietnamese took it to new heights with their unique brewing techniques and flavours. French pastries, such as croissants and éclairs, have also found a special place in Vietnamese bakeries, often enjoyed alongside a cup of robust Vietnamese coffee.

In this culinary journey, I've used mussels to guide you along the French flavour trail, tracing the rich and diverse influences of French cuisine from its origins in Provence to its colonial imprints in Pondicherry and Phan Thiet. Mussels, a staple in French coastal regions, serve as a delicious medium to explore the fusion of French techniques and local ingredients. Whether it's a traditional **Moules à la Provençale**, a South Indian **Spicy Mussels Fry**, or Vietnamese **Mussels with Chilli, Lime, and Coconut**, each dish tells a story of cultural exchange and culinary adaptation. This journey highlights the enduring legacy of French culinary tradition and its ability to blend seamlessly with local flavours, creating dishes that are both familiar and uniquely exciting.

MOULES À LA PROVENÇALE (PROVENÇAL MUSSELS)

France

Prep time: 20 minutes | Cooking time: 20 minutes | Serves 4

Moules à la Provençale, translating to 'Mussels in the Provençal style', typically includes fresh mussels cooked in a flavourful tomato-based sauce with a variety of herbs. The dish originates from the Provence region of southern France, which is known for its Mediterranean cuisine and fresh ingredients.

The dish can be served as an appetiser or main course and is often enjoyed with crusty bread to help soak up its delicious sauce.

1kg fresh mussels, in shells

2 tbsp olive oil

1 onion, chopped

3 cloves of garlic, finely chopped

1 large tomato, chopped

125ml white wine

2 tbsp fresh herbs, chopped (such as oregano or basil)

3 tbsp fresh parsley, chopped, plus extra to garnish

Salt and pepper, to taste

Scrub and debeard the mussels, discarding any that are already open and do not close when tapped.

In a large pot, heat the olive oil over a medium heat, then sauté the onion and garlic for 5 minutes until softened. Stir in the chopped tomato and cook for another 5 minutes, then add the mussels, white wine, fresh herbs, salt, and pepper.

Cover the pot and cook for 8 to 10 minutes until the mussels open, making sure to discard any mussels that remain closed. Garnish with extra chopped fresh parsley and serve immediately with crusty bread to soak up the delicious sauce.

SPICY MUSSELS FRY

India

Prep time: 25 minutes | Cooking time: 25 minutes | Serves 4

This flavourful and aromatic dish is from the coastal state of Kerala in India. It features tender marinated mussels sautéed with a fragrant blend of onions, green chillies, ginger, garlic, and curry leaves. The addition of tamarind paste infuses the mussels with a tangy richness. Finished with a garnish of fresh coriander, this spicy delicacy is best enjoyed as an appetiser or side dish with rice or bread.

500g mussels, cleaned (weighed without shells)
1 tbsp lemon juice
Salt, to taste
1 tsp turmeric
1 tbsp tamarind paste, or a 1-inch ball of tamarind
2 tbsp coconut oil
1 large onion, finely sliced
2-3 green chillies, sliced in half

10-12 curry leaves
1-inch piece of ginger, minced
5-6 cloves of garlic, minced
1 tsp black pepper
1 tsp ground coriander
1 large tomato, chopped
1 handful of fresh coriander leaves, chopped, to garnish

Marinate the cleaned mussels in a bowl with the lemon juice, salt, and turmeric. Set aside for 10 minutes to allow the flavours to meld.

If using whole tamarind, soak the ball of tamarind in 60ml of warm water for 10 minutes. Extract the pulp, discard the seeds and fibres, and set aside.

Heat the coconut oil in a large pan over a medium heat, then add the sliced onions and green chillies. Sauté for 8 to 10 minutes until the onions turn golden-brown. Add the curry leaves, ginger and garlic and sauté for another 3 to 4 minutes. Stir in the pepper and coriander and cook for a further minute.

Add the chopped tomato and cook for 6 to 8 minutes before stirring the tamarind paste or pulp through. Add the marinated mussels to the pan and mix to coat them with the spices. Keep on a medium heat for 5 to 6 minutes, stirring occasionally, until the mussels are cooked through. Garnish with fresh coriander leaves then serve with rice, bread or parathas.

MUSSELS WITH CHILLI, LIME AND COCONUT

Vietnam

Prep time: 20 minutes | Cooking time: 20 minutes | Serves 4

These Vietnamese-style mussels are cooked in a fragrant blend of sweet coconut milk and citrusy lemongrass. The rich, aromatic broth perfectly complements the fresh mussels, and the addition of garlic, ginger, and a hint of chilli bring complexity and a subtle kick.

These can be enjoyed as a main course or appetiser, and this dish pairs well with steamed jasmine rice or crusty bread to soak up the delicious broth.

1kg fresh mussels, in shells

2 tbsp vegetable oil

1 large onion, finely chopped

2 cloves of garlic, minced

1-inch piece of ginger, minced

2 lemongrass stalks, trimmed and finely chopped (white part only)

2 red chillies, finely chopped (adjust to taste)

½ tin of coconut milk (200ml)

125ml chicken or vegetable stock

2 tbsp fish sauce

1 lime, juiced

1 tsp white sugar

30g fresh coriander, chopped, plus extra to garnish

15g basil leaves, plus extra to garnish

Lime wedges, to serve

Clean and debeard the mussels, then discard any mussels that are already open and do not close when tapped.

Warm the oil in a large pot over a medium heat. Add the chopped onion, garlic, ginger, lemongrass, and red chillies, and sauté for 2 to 3 minutes until fragrant.

Pour in the coconut milk and chicken or vegetable stock, then stir in the fish sauce, lime juice and sugar. Reduce to a simmer for 5 minutes.

Add the cleaned mussels to the pot, then cover and cook for 8 to 10 minutes, or until the mussels open. Make sure to discard any mussels that do not open, then stir in the chopped coriander and basil leaves.

Scoop the mussels and broth into bowls, then garnish with additional fresh herbs and lime wedges to serve.

NOODLES

NOODLE TRAILS

THAILAND, TIBET, AND INDIA (ALSO MYANMAR)

In this section, we delve into more recent historical events that have shaped the journey of noodles and their culinary use in India, Southeast Asia, and Myanmar (formerly Burma). As we explore the dynamic interplay of political shifts, cultural exchanges, and migration patterns, we uncover new dimensions of this beloved dish's evolution.

India, Thailand, and Myanmar have historically shared close links due to extensive maritime trade routes and the overland Silk Road. Increased interaction between India and Southeast Asia during the British colonial period meant British administrators and soldiers, who had experienced Chinese cuisine in other parts of the British Empire, such as Hong Kong and Singapore, brought these culinary influences back to India. The movement of people between India, Myanmar, and Thailand further contributed to the sharing of culinary traditions. For example, the migration of Indian and Chinese communities to Myanmar and Thailand introduced dishes like paratha and noodles, such as the stir fried Pad Kee Mao (**Drunken Noodles**) which was later adapted to suit local Thai tastes.

In the late 19th and early 20th centuries, Chinese immigrants settled in various parts of India, notably in Kolkata (formerly Calcutta). These immigrants established Chinatown in Kolkata, where they introduced Chinese culinary traditions, including noodles, to the local population. This led to the development of unique Indo-Chinese cuisine. Over time, the Indian adaptation of Chinese noodles evolved into a distinct style known as Indo-Chinese cuisine. Dishes like Hakka Noodles and Chow Mein became popular, incorporating Indian spices and ingredients like green chillies, garlic, ginger, and various Indian spices, creating a hotter and more robust version that appealed to Indian tastes.

What I find fascinating is the journey of noodles and how this has been shaped by the political history and immigration between India and Myanmar. Although trade and cultural relations between India and Myanmar have been in development since ancient times, and migration from India was a prominent and continuous feature of Indo-Burmese contact in pre-colonial days, the beginning of Indian immigration on an appreciable scale began in 1852 during colonial rule. After 1852, Indians migrated to what was then lower Burma in large numbers to fill a wide range of jobs created by the expanding economy. This continued until the British separated the Burma province from India in 1937.

In the early 1960s, amidst political upheaval and military rule in Burma, significant changes prompted the repatriation of Indian-origin Burmese communities. The repatriated Burmese Indians found refuge and resettlement support in Tamil Nadu, where there were existing cultural and linguistic ties. The Rangoon-returned traders set up what is still called Burma Bazaar, a market where **Atho Noodles** are a popular dish sold at Burmese food stalls. Atho is essentially a noodle salad, and it has adapted — as dishes often do when transplanted to a new setting — to fit in with local Indian tastes and produce.

Another noodle dish that has crossed boundaries and found popularity in India is **Thukpa**, a traditional Tibetan noodle soup. The love for this dish is deeply rooted in the migration of Tibetan people to India and the cultural exchange that followed. It gained popularity after many Tibetans migrated to India, particularly following the 1959 Tibetan uprising against Chinese rule. It is now common in regions like Ladakh and Himachal Pradesh, where there are close cultural and historical ties to Tibet, showing how we can form strong cultural bonds through a love of good food.

YUI'S DRUNKEN NOODLES (PAD KEE MAO)
Thailand

Prep time: 15 minutes | Cooking time: 25 minutes | Serves 2

"Drunken Noodles, or Pad Kee Mao, is a flavourful, tasty dish made with rice noodles stir fried with a combination of meat, seafood or tofu with vegetables, chilli, Thai basil and young green peppercorns. This well-known Thai street food gets its name from the idea that it's a great cure for a hangover." - Yui Miles, @cookingwith_yui

I want to say a big thank you to my friend Yui Miles for sharing this delicious recipe. I have been a huge fan of her Thai cooking ever since I saw her on MasterChef in 2019. Her culinary skills and creativity continue to inspire me, and I am grateful for her generosity in sharing her expertise.

200g dry flat rice noodles

3-4 tbsp vegetable oil

2 cloves of garlic, finely chopped

150g chicken, cut into bite-sized pieces

1 red chilli, thinly sliced

1 onion, finely sliced

1 handful of green beans, cut into 3cm-long pieces

4-5 baby corn, cut in half

2-3 bunches young green peppercorns (or 1-2 tbsp of green peppercorns in brine)

2 handfuls of Thai basil

Pinch of white pepper, to taste

FOR THE SAUCE

2 tbsp light soy sauce

2 tbsp oyster sauce

1 tbsp fish sauce

2 tbsp brown sugar

Soak the rice noodles in warm water for about 15 minutes or until the noodles have softened. Drain the water and set aside. Meanwhile, mix all the sauce ingredients together in a separate bowl and set aside.

Warm the vegetable oil in a pan or wok over a medium heat, then add the garlic, stir quickly, and sauté until golden-brown. Add the diced chicken and stir. Once the chicken is about 70% of the way cooked, add the red chilli, onion, green beans, and baby corn. Stir fry for 2 to 3 minutes.

Add the rice noodles and sauce and stir well to coat. Add 2 to 3 tablespoons of water, if needed, to reach the desired consistency. Stir in the young green peppercorns and Thai basil, then remove from the heat and sprinkle with some white pepper before serving.

THUPKA NOODLE SOUP
Tibet

Prep time: 25 minutes | Cooking time: 20 minutes | Serves 4

Thukpa is a traditional noodle soup originating from Tibet which is popular in Nepal, Bhutan, and the Indian Himalayan regions. It's made with noodles, vegetables, and sometimes meat or fish, all cooked in a flavourful broth. The recipe can be customised with a variety of ingredients, making it a versatile and nutritious option for a midweek meal.

I used to enjoy Thukpa during my college days in Delhi. There was a significant Tibetan community in the city, and refugees would prepare this delicious dish along with momos (a type of dumpling). Memories of cold Delhi winters, where I'd savour hot Thukpa with fiery chilli paste and momo chutney, remain strong and vivid; a touch of nostalgia warming those chilly days.

200g wheat noodles

2 tbsp vegetable oil

1-inch piece of ginger, finely chopped

5 cloves of garlic, finely chopped

2 green chillies, cut diagonally

1 medium onion, thinly sliced

1 large tomato, sliced

½ tsp turmeric

1 tsp chilli powder

½ tsp ground cumin

1 tsp garam masala

Sichuan peppercorns, ground, to taste

1L vegetable stock or hot water

1 carrot, julienned

2 peppers, julienned (1 red, 1 green)

50g cabbage, shredded

1 tbsp soy sauce

Salt, to taste

1 tbsp vinegar, or 1 tbsp lime juice

15g fresh coriander leaves, chopped, plus extra to garnish

2-3 spring onions, finely chopped

Chilli oil, to serve (optional)

Cook the noodles as per the packet instructions, then drain, drizzle with a little oil to prevent them sticking together, and set aside.

Heat the vegetable oil in a wok, then add the ginger, garlic, and chillies. Cook on a high heat for 1 minute before adding the sliced onions. Sauté for a couple of minutes, then add the tomatoes and cook for a further minute.

Add the ground spices and cook for one minute, then pour in the stock and bring to boil. Once boiling, add all the vegetables, soy sauce and salt. Stir well and cook for 2 to 3 minutes.

Finally, add the vinegar or lime juice, coriander, and spring onions. Ladle the hot broth over the noodles in large, deep bowls, then garnish with extra coriander leaves and/or chilli oil and serve.

ATHO NOODLES

India

Prep time: 15 minutes | Cooking time: 20 minutes | Serves 4 (as a side or snack)

Atho Noodles are a popular Burmese street food in Chennai, South India. The dish is made using a blend of boiled noodles mixed with cabbage, green chillies, fried onions, garlic, and a variety of seasonings. It is a spicy, tangy, and nutty dish, like a crunchy noodle chaat, combining a variety of textures and flavours to make a delightful and unique street food experience.

After tasting these noodles during my travels in South India, I was so curious to explore the history behind them. Atho Noodles, originally from Myanmar (Burma), were brought to Chennai by Burmese refugees in the 1960s and have seamlessly integrated into the local food culture of Chennai. This recipe now commonly incorporates classic Indian ingredients like tamarind juice, spicy chilli sauce, curry leaves, and a kick of Kashmiri chilli. In Myanmar, these noodles are typically eaten with Egg Bhejo (see page 140).

250g wheat noodles

30g unsalted peanuts

2-3 dried red chillies

4 tbsp vegetable oil

8 curry leaves, plus 6-8, fried, to garnish

2 red onions. thinly sliced

8-10 cloves of garlic, finely chopped

225g green cabbage, shredded

2 green chillies, chopped

1 tbsp Kashmiri chilli powder

Salt, to taste

1 lemon, juiced

2 tbsp tamarind juice (1 golf ball-sized piece of tamarind soaked in 125ml water for 10-15 minutes, strained, and juice extracted)

¼ tsp white sugar

2 tbsp fried onions (shop-bought)

Cook the noodles as per to the packet instructions, then drain and set aside. Toss with a little oil to prevent them sticking together.

Dry roast the peanuts and red chillies, then coarsely pound them in a pestle and mortar and set aside.

Heat 4 tablespoons of oil in a wok. Fry 6 to 8 curry leaves and set aside for the garnish, then add the remaining curry leaves, sliced onion, garlic, and shredded cabbage and cook on a high heat for 2 minutes. The vegetables should not be overcooked, as this dish is meant to have a crunchy texture.

Add the green chillies, Kashmiri chilli powder, salt and cooked noodles. Toss well to coat, then remove from the heat. Add the lemon, tamarind juice, sugar, ground peanuts and mix well.

Garnish with fried onions and the reserved crispy curry leaves, then serve warm or at room temperature.

CHICKEN

SPIRITUAL AND CULINARY JOURNEYS

CAMBODIA, MALAYSIA, AND INDIA

The culinary connections between India, Cambodia, and Malaysia have deep historical roots, primarily facilitated by ancient trade routes, cultural exchanges, and the spread of Hinduism and Buddhism from India to Southeast Asia. These interactions led to the blending of flavours, ingredients, and cooking techniques across these regions.

India's influence on Cambodian cuisine is largely linked to the spread of Hinduism and later Buddhism, which brought with it cultural exchange as well as Indian spices, ingredients, and cooking techniques. The Khmer Empire, which ruled much of Southeast Asia from the 9th to the 15th century, had significant trade and cultural ties with India. This led to the adoption of Indian spices, cooking techniques, and ingredients in Cambodian cuisine, resulting in dishes like **Chicken Samla Curry** that showcase a fusion of flavours from both regions. This is a traditional Cambodian curry that features a rich and aromatic blend of spices, coconut milk, and often includes ingredients like lemongrass and kaffir lime leaves. The use of coconut milk and spices like turmeric and cardamom reflect the Indian culinary influence.

The culinary history and influences between India and Malaysia are also deeply intertwined, shaped by centuries of trade, migration, and cultural exchange. Besides the ancient historical trade connections that linked the Indian subcontinent with Southeast Asia, Indian traders and merchants, particularly those from South India, played a crucial role in the spread of Indian spices, cooking techniques, and religious practices to the Malay Peninsula. The British colonial period further strengthened these connections as large numbers of Indian labourers were brought to Malaysia, particularly from Tamil Nadu, which led to the establishment of vibrant Indian communities. Spices like cumin, coriander, turmeric, and fennel, which are staples in Indian kitchens, became integral to Malaysian dishes like Nasi Kandar and **Rendang**. Indian breads, particularly roti canai (a flaky flatbread similar to the Indian paratha), have become a staple in Malaysian cuisine and are often served with daal (lentil curry).

Dahi Chicken is a dish made by marinating chicken in yoghurt and a blend of spices such as cumin, coriander, and turmeric. The yoghurt tenderises the meat and adds a tangy richness to the dish. While Dahi Chicken is distinctly Indian, the practice of using yoghurt in cooking and marination is not unique to India. Similar techniques are found in other cuisines across the Middle East, Greece, and Southeast Asia, where yoghurt or other fermented products are used to tenderise meat and enhance its flavour.

This collection of chicken dishes highlights the rich connections between these three countries and others beyond them. Their shared appreciation of spices connects them across borders, highlighting the fascinating impact that the expansion of industry, religion, and trade can have on a country's cuisine.

CHICKEN SAMLA CURRY
Cambodia

Prep time: 15 minutes | Cooking time: 40 minutes | Serves 4

Samla Curry is a wonderfully delicate and aromatic traditional Cambodian dish that pairs perfectly with steamed white rice. This dish has a soupy and creamy texture thanks to the richness of the coconut milk as well as a distinctive flavour profile from the blend of aromatics.

The dish can also be enriched with a variety of vegetables, such as purple sweet potatoes, bamboo shoots, green beans, and spinach. It's an absolute must-try for those who appreciate the nuanced and delicate flavours of South Asian curries.

FOR THE CURRY PASTE

3 lemongrass stalks

6 cloves of garlic

2-inch piece of galangal or fresh ginger, peeled and chopped

2 red chillies (adjust according to taste)

2-3 kaffir lime leaves

1 tsp shrimp paste

3-4 tbsp water

FOR THE CURRY SAUCE

750g chicken thighs

1 tsp turmeric powder

1 x 400ml tin of coconut milk

4-5 tbsp vegetable oil

2 tbsp fish sauce

¼ tsp sugar

Salt, to taste

2 tbsp coriander leaves, chopped, to garnish

To prepare the curry paste, add all the paste ingredients to a blender and blitz until smooth.

Coat the chicken pieces with the turmeric and set aside (add a drop of oil, if required, to allow the turmeric to stick). Heat the oil in a large casserole dish, then add the chicken pieces to the pot and cook until browned on all sides, about 10 minutes.

Drain any excess oil and add the curry paste, then mix well and cook on a medium heat for 4 to 6 minutes. Add the coconut milk, fish sauce and sugar and stir well to combine.

Bring to the boil, then reduce to a simmer for about 20 to 25 minutes, or until the chicken is cooked through. Season to taste with some salt.

Garnish with fresh coriander and serve hot with steamed jasmine rice or whichever rice you prefer.

ZALEHA'S CHICKEN RENDANG
Malaysia

Prep time: 30 minutes | Cooking time: 1 hour 30 minutes | Serves 6

This simplified Chicken Rendang recipe is a quick and convenient take on a beloved Malaysian dish. With tender chicken cooked in a blend of chillies, lemongrass, and galangal, it effortlessly captures the essence of Malaysian cuisine. The defining aroma of a rendang is the turmeric leaves, but they're difficult to find in the UK. You can substitute them with more kaffir lime leaves.

A special thanks to my dear friend Zaleha (@zaleha.olpin) for sharing this recipe. Zaleha was a quarterfinalist on MasterChef in 2018 and is fondly known as "That Rendang Lady" (following her controversial elimination episode). Thank you, Zaleha, for bringing a touch of your MasterChef magic to my kitchen!

FOR THE SPICE PASTE
185g onions, roughly chopped
20g ginger, roughly chopped
15g garlic, roughly chopped
15g galangal, roughly chopped
50g red chillies, roughly chopped

FOR THE SAUCE
60ml vegetable oil
15g lemongrass stalks, outer layer discarded
½ tbsp medium chilli powder (add more if you want it spicier)
2 tsp turmeric
300ml coconut milk

1-2 pieces of tamarind skin or dried tamarind slices
6-8 kaffir lime leaves
1.2kg whole chicken, cut into 8 pieces
45g toasted desiccated coconut
1-2 turmeric leaves, cut into ribbons (or more kaffir lime leaves)

Place all the spice paste ingredients into a blender and blitz to a coarse paste. Place the oil into a shallow casserole dish or wok and heat on a low-medium flame. Once hot, add the blended spice paste. Using the back of a knife or a pestle, bruise the ends of the lemongrass stalks then add them to the pot.

Fry the paste for 12 to 15 minutes or until fragrant and the oil starts to split. Stir frequently to avoid burning the paste and add more oil if necessary.

Add the chilli powder and turmeric and continue cooking the paste for another 5 minutes. Once the oil has separated again, add the coconut milk, tamarind skin and kaffir lime leaves. Cover with a lid and reduce to a simmer for 20 minutes, stirring frequently.

Once the sauce has thickened slightly, add the chicken, toasted desiccated coconut and turmeric (or lime) leaves. Stir to coat the chicken in the sauce, then place the lid on again and simmer for another 35 to 40 minutes, or until the chicken is fully cooked and the sauce has thickened.

You can take the rendang off the heat after the chicken is cooked, but if you prefer a drier rendang then continue cooking the sauce to your desired thickness. Serve with plain or coconut rice.

NOTE

Ensure the oil has split before adding the coconut milk – this shows that the spice paste has cooked through properly.

MANNA'S DAHI TAMATAR CHICKEN (CHICKEN COOKED IN A YOGHURT AND TOMATO SAUCE)

India

Prep time: 15 minutes, plus 3 hours marinating | Cooking time: 45 minutes | Serves 4

This chicken curry recipe is my creation and I often make it for my nephew, Yaamir, who affectionately calls me "Manna." Whenever he comes home, I prepare this delicious and fuss-free recipe for him, bringing joy and comfort to our family meals. The creamy and tangy flavours of this dish make it one of Yaamir's favourites. It can be enjoyed with rice, naans, or any flatbread.

FOR THE MARINADE

6 tbsp Greek yoghurt

½ tsp ground cumin

1 tsp ground coriander

½ tsp turmeric

¼ tsp red chilli powder

2 tsp ginger paste

2 tsp garlic paste

1 tsp dried mint

1 tsp garam masala

Salt, to taste

FOR THE DISH

750g boneless chicken thighs

3 tbsp vegetable oil

2 bay leaves

1-inch cinnamon stick

4-5 green cardamom pods

1 black cardamom pods

1 x 400g tin of chopped tomatoes, blended

1 tsp turmeric

Salt, to taste

1 tsp kasuri methi (dried fenugreek leaves)

2 tbsp coriander leaves, to garnish

Combine the marinade ingredients, then add to the chicken and stir to coat. Cover and refrigerate for 2 to 3 hours, or overnight for best results.

Heat the oil in a large pan over medium heat. Add the bay leaves, cinnamon stick, and green and black cardamom pods. Fry gently until fragrant, then add the tomatoes, mix well, and cook on low heat for 10 minutes.

Add the turmeric, salt, and marinated chicken (including the marinade) to the pan. Cook on a medium-high heat, stirring occasionally, until the chicken is browned on all sides, about 10 minutes. Then, reduce the heat to low, cover the pan, and let the chicken simmer for about 20 to 25 minutes, or until it is fully cooked and tender.

Crush the kasuri methi between your palms before adding them to the chicken, then garnish with coriander leaves and serve.

CHICKPEAS

THE CHICKPEA CONNECTION

INDIA, TUNISIA, AND SPAIN

Chickpeas have a long and fascinating history that connects India, the Maghreb region, and Spain through trade routes and cultural exchanges, particularly along the Silk Road. The Silk Road, an ancient network of trade routes connecting the East and West, played a significant role in the exchange of goods, including agricultural products like chickpeas. Through these trade routes, chickpeas were introduced to India from the Middle East and the Mediterranean, becoming a staple in Indian agriculture and cuisine.

Chickpeas are believed to have originated in the Mediterranean region and have been cultivated since ancient times. They were introduced to North Africa, including Tunisia, through trade routes that connected the Mediterranean world with the Middle East and beyond. In India, chickpeas, known as 'chana' or 'chole', became a core ingredient in various regional cuisines, particularly in North and South Indian dishes. One of these dishes is the delicious **Mangalorean Chickpea Ghassi**.

In North African cuisine, including Tunisian cuisine, chickpeas feature in a variety of dishes such as couscous, stews, salads, and soups like **Lablabi**. While direct historical records of chickpea trade between India and the Maghreb region may be limited, the broader historical and cultural connections between these regions through trade and migration routes suggest that chickpeas were likely introduced and integrated into local cuisines through these interactions.

Chickpeas, or 'garbanzo' in Spanish, are believed to have been introduced to Spain by the Moors during their rule from the 8th to the 15th centuries. They also introduced ingredients like cumin, which later became an integral component of many Spanish dishes. These ingredients, along with the use of garlic and olive oil, can be seen in **Garbanzos con Espinacas**, a dish resulting from the harmonious blending of Moorish and Spanish culinary traditions.

NANI'S CHANA GHASSI

India

Prep time: 15 minutes (plus overnight soaking, if using dried chickpeas) | Cooking time: 35 minutes (1 hour 25 minutes, or 50 minutes with a pressure cooker if using dried chickpeas) | Serves 4

Chana Gassi, also spelled 'ghassi' or 'gashi', is a popular Mangalorean curry dish from Karnataka, India. It consists of chickpeas and yams in a thick coconut-based gravy, flavoured with freshly ground spices and tamarind. It is the quintessential dish of the Konkan region and its Konkani community, representing the vibrant culinary landscape that spans across the western coast of India, including Goa and Karnataka.

This recipe holds a special place in my heart and is inspired by my grandmother's heritage. She introduced me to the vibrant world of Mangalorean cuisine, with its unique blend of flavours and ingredients. She had a contagious passion for cooking and always took pride in sharing her culinary knowledge with me.

175g dried chickpeas or
2 x 400g tins of chickpeas

FOR THE MASALA PASTE

1 tsp vegetable oil

4 dried red chillies

2 tsp coriander seeds

½ tsp cumin seeds

¼ tsp black mustard seeds

4 black peppercorns

2 cloves

1 tsp turmeric

1 golf-sized ball of tamarind, soaked in 125ml warm water for 15 minutes, juice extracted from the pulp

FOR THE GRAVY

2 tbsp vegetable oil

6-8 curry leaves

2 white onions, finely chopped

1 tbsp ginger paste

1 tbsp garlic paste

Salt, to taste

1 x 400ml tin of coconut milk

If using dried chickpeas, soak them in a large bowl of water for 8 hours or overnight (making sure the water covers them). Then, cook the chickpeas with the water in a pan until they have softened - this can take about 45 to 50 minutes. Alternatively, drain the chickpeas and rinse well, then place them in a pressure cooker with 750ml of water and a pinch of salt. Cook for 15 minutes, then set aside with the cooking liquid.

To make the masala spice paste, heat the oil in a pan and add the red chillies, coriander seeds, cumin seeds, mustard seeds, peppercorns, and cloves. Sauté for 1 minute on a medium heat until fragrant, then set aside to cool. Add the sautéed spices, turmeric and tamarind extract to a pestle and mortar and grind to a smooth paste. Add 125ml of water and stir to combine.

To make the gravy, add the oil to a large cooking pot along with the curry leaves and onions and sauté for 10 minutes until the onions turn golden-brown. Add the ginger and garlic pastes and cook for a further 5 minutes on a medium heat. Add the masala paste and cook for 4 to 5 minutes, then season to taste with salt.

Add the cooked chickpeas (from earlier or directly from the tin) and mix well. Pour in the coconut milk, bring to the boil, and simmer on a low heat for 10 to 12 minutes. Add 250ml water to loosen the sauce, if necessary.

Mash some of the chickpeas with a potato masher or back of a spoon to give the curry a creamier texture. Serve hot with rice or rotis.

NOTE

You can temper the dish with one teaspoon of ghee and 5-6 curry leaves to further enhance the flavours.

LABLABI CHICKPEA STEW

Tunisia

Prep time: 15 minutes | Cooking time: 45 minutes (1 hour 40 minutes, if using dried chickpeas) | Serves 4

Lablabi is a traditional Tunisian chickpea soup or stew, commonly enjoyed as a hearty and comforting street food. The dish primarily consists of tender cooked chickpeas served in a flavourful broth that's typically been seasoned with cumin, garlic, and harissa (a spicy North African chilli paste).

Lablabi is often served over small pieces of stale crusty bread with a generous drizzle of extra-virgin olive oil. It can be garnished with a variety of toppings, such as chopped hard-boiled eggs, olives, capers, or preserved lemon. These toppings add texture, colour, and additional layers of flavour to the dish.

3 x 400g tins of chickpeas, or 175g dried chickpeas, soaked overnight

1.5L water, or 2L if using dried chickpeas

3 tbsp olive oil, plus extra to serve

1 bay leaf

1 large onion, finely chopped

1 tsp cumin seeds

6-8 garlic cloves, minced

1 tsp ground cumin

1 tsp ground coriander

1 tsp paprika

Salt and pepper, to taste

2 tbsp harissa paste (adjust to taste)

1 lemon, juiced

½ loaf of crusty bread, torn into large chunks

4 eggs, hard-boiled, to garnish

30g fresh parsley, chopped, to garnish

1 tbsp capers, to garnish

If using pre-soaked dried chickpeas, drain and transfer to a large pot. Cover with 2 litres of water and bring to the boil. Reduce to a simmer for about an hour until the chickpeas are tender. If using tinned chickpeas, empty into a cooking pot, cover with 1.5 litres of water, and bring the chickpeas to the boil. Lower the heat and simmer the chickpeas for about 20 minutes, until soft and tender.

In a separate pan, heat the olive oil and add the bay leaf, onions, cumin seeds and garlic. Sauté on medium heat for 10 minutes before adding the ground cumin, coriander, paprika, salt, and pepper. Cook for 2 minutes then add the spiced, sautéed onions to the pot of simmering chickpeas.

Add the harissa paste and lemon juice and simmer for a further 10 minutes. Check the liquid in the pan: there should be enough to cover the chickpeas by 1-inch. Add another cup (250ml) of water if there is not enough liquid.

Toss the torn bread in olive oil and spread the pieces over a baking sheet. Toast the bread under a hot grill for 2 to 3 minutes or until the bread turns golden-brown. To serve, place the toasted bread pieces in a bowl and ladle the chickpea soup over the bread. Top with boiled eggs, chopped parsley, capers and a drizzle of olive oil, or your choice of toppings.

NOTE

For a richer and more complex flavour, consider adding a bit of preserved lemon or a spoonful of olive tapenade as a topping.

GARBANZOS CON ESPINACAS (CHICKPEA AND SPINACH STEW)

Spain

Prep time: 15 minutes | Cooking time: 50 minutes | Serves 4

Garbanzos con Espinacas is a traditional Spanish dish originating from the Andalusian region, which is renowned for its rich culinary heritage. The term 'garbanzo' in Spanish means chickpeas, and this dish is a wonderful example of the Moorish influence on Spanish cuisine. The use of chickpeas and cumin, both introduced by the Moors, is central to the dish, and the slow-cooking method reflects Moorish culinary traditions. Spinach was also introduced to Spain by Arab traders, so this dish is a great demonstration of cross-cultural trade and culinary inspiration.

This recipe comes from my Spanish family and has been an all-time family favourite. Whether served as a main course or as a hearty side, Garbanzos con Espinacas embodies the essence of Spanish home cooking and continues to be a favourite in households worldwide.

5-6 tbsp olive oil

2 slices white bread, crusts removed, cut into small chunks

30g blanched almonds

1 tsp cumin seeds

1 tsp smoked paprika

1 large onion, thinly sliced

6 cloves of garlic, finely chopped

2 tbsp tomato purée

1 x 400g tin of chopped tomatoes

2 x 400g tins chickpeas

2 tbsp red wine vinegar

10-12 saffron threads, brewed in 2 tbsp of warm water for 10 minutes

150g spinach, washed

Salt and pepper, to taste

Extra-virgin olive oil, to serve

Heat 2 tablespoons of olive oil in a frying pan over a medium heat and fry the bread chunks for 3 to 4 minutes until lightly browned. Add the almonds, cumin seeds and smoked paprika and toast for 1 minute. Transfer everything to a food processor and blend to form a paste. Add a little water to thin the mixture and blend again.

In a separate, deep pan, heat 3 tablespoons of olive oil and gently cook the onion for 10 minutes until softened. Add the garlic, tomato purée and tomatoes and season well. Simmer for 20 minutes and add a little water if you find the sauce is sticking to the base of the pan.

Add the chickpeas (along with the liquid from the tin) and simmer for a further 10 minutes.

Mash some of the chickpeas in the pan to enhance the creaminess of the dish, then add the bread paste and bring to the boil. Add the vinegar and saffron and simmer for a few minutes to thicken, then tip in the spinach and stir until fully combined. Season with salt and pepper to taste, then serve in small bowls and drizzle with extra-virgin olive oil.

LENTILS

THE LOVE OF LENTILS

GREECE, PAKISTAN, AND INDIA

The shared history of brown lentils across Pakistan, Greece, and India underscores the profound impact of ancient trade routes and cultural exchanges. Through Alexander the Great's campaigns and the subsequent blending of cultures, the use of lentils became a shared element of the diets and culinary identities of these regions.

Alexander the Great's campaigns in the Indus Valley significantly influenced cultural exchanges between Greece and South Asia and contributed to the spread of agricultural products like lentils. When Alexander entered the Indus Valley around 327 BCE, his campaigns facilitated a flow of goods, ideas, and practices between the Greeks and the local populations, including the blending of Greek and South Asian art, philosophy, and agricultural techniques. This blending was particularly visible in the Greco-Buddhist art of the Gandhara region.

Brown lentils have become a significant part of Greek cuisine. They are commonly used in soups, stews, and salads, such as **Lentil and Feta Salad**, and are appreciated for their earthy flavour and versatility. Greek lentil soup, known as 'fakes', is a traditional, widely eaten dish that highlights the prominence of lentils in Greek cooking.

Lentils also have a rich history in both India and Pakistan, with evidence of lentil cultivation dating back thousands of years to the Indus Valley Civilisation, which encompassed parts of modern-day India and Pakistan. Despite their shared history and culinary traditions, India and Pakistan have developed distinct regional flavours and cooking styles that make their lentil dishes unique and delicious.

Pakistani cuisine often features a culinary technique that involves cooking meat with lentils, creating rich dishes like the much-loved **Qeema Masoor**. The practice of combining meat and lentils can be traced back to the Mughal Empire, which ruled over much of present-day Pakistan and India from the 16th to 19th centuries.

Lentils, otherwise known as daal, hold a special place in Indian cuisine, serving as the soul and foundation of countless traditional dishes. Different regions of India have developed unique lentil dishes, from the spicy Sambar of South India to the creamy Daal Makhani of North India. They can be prepared in a myriad of ways, from a simple daal (lentil soup) to more wholesome dishes like **Masoor Spinach Daal**, where brown lentils are cooked with spinach to create a nutritious and flavourful meal.

LENTIL AND FETA SALAD

Greece

Prep time: 15 minutes (plus 2 hours soaking) | Cooking time: 30 minutes | Serves 4

This Greek lentil salad is a vibrant and nutritious dish that combines the hearty texture of brown lentils with the fresh flavours of a traditional Greek salad. Featuring crumbled feta cheese, juicy cherry tomatoes, crisp cucumber, sweet red pepper, and tangy red onion, this salad is dressed in a savoury mix of olive oil, red wine vinegar, and tahini with a touch of garlic and dried oregano.

Perfect as a main course or a side dish, this salad is both delicious and satisfying, offering a delightful blend of Mediterranean flavours.

200g dried brown lentils, washed and soaked in water for 1 to 2 hours

150g feta cheese

150g cherry tomatoes, halved

½ cucumber, chopped

1 red pepper, chopped

1 red onion, sliced

4 tbsp olive oil

2 tbsp red wine vinegar

2 tbsp tahini

2 cloves of garlic, minced

1 tsp dried oregano

Salt and pepper, to taste

15g fresh parsley, chopped

10g fresh dill

20g pistachios, chopped

1 tsp red chilli flakes

Add 750ml water to a large pot and bring to the boil. Add the rinsed, soaked lentils to the boiling water, reduce to a simmer, and cook, uncovered, for about 20 to 25 minutes. The lentils should be tender but not mushy. Drain any excess water if necessary and allow to cool.

In a large bowl, combine the cooked lentils with the crumbled feta cheese, cherry tomatoes, cucumber, red pepper, and red onion. Then, in a separate small bowl, whisk together the olive oil, red wine vinegar, tahini, minced garlic, and dried oregano until well combined.

Pour the dressing over the salad and toss well to combine all ingredients. Season with salt and pepper to taste, then sprinkle over the fresh herbs, pistachios and chilli flakes.

NOTE

The cooking time of lentils can vary significantly depending on how long they have been soaked. Pre-soaking lentils can reduce the cooking time and help achieve a more even texture. For best results, adjust the cooking time based on the specific type of lentil and their soaking duration.

SAYEEDA'S QEEMA MASOOR (LENTILS WITH MINCE)

Pakistan

Prep time: 20 minutes | Cooking time: 40 minutes | Serves 4-6

Qeema Masoor is a unique and flavourful dish that combines minced meat with lentils. This dish is enriched with aromatic spices, fresh mint, and creamy yoghurt. The combination of tender minced meat and lentils, simmered in a spiced gravy, results in a rich and comforting dish that is perfect for any occasion. The addition of mint and yoghurt adds a refreshing and tangy twist.

This recipe is a cherished gift from my dear old neighbour, Sayeeda. At age 85, she was an extraordinary cook, and I was incredibly fortunate to learn some authentic Pakistani recipes from her. Each time I make this dish, I'm reminded of her generous spirit and the invaluable lessons she shared with me.

This dish can be enjoyed as a main course with rice, naan, or parathas.

500g lamb mince

200g dried brown lentils, washed and soaked in water for 1-2 hours

2 tbsp ginger paste

2 tbsp garlic paste

2 green chillies, crushed (optional)

2 tsp chilli powder

1 tsp turmeric

2 tsp ground coriander

1 tsp ground cumin

1 tsp garam masala

Salt, to taste

250g Greek yoghurt

2 tbsp biryani masala (store-bought)

2 tbsp fresh coriander, chopped

2 tbsp fresh mint leaves, chopped

2 tbsp lemon juice

3 medium tomatoes, chopped

85g fried onions (store-bought)

6 tbsp vegetable oil

1-inch cinnamon stick

4 cloves

1 black cardamom pod

2-3 green cardamom pods

750ml water

TO SERVE

1 handful of fresh coriander, chopped

1 handful of fresh mint, chopped

2 tbsp fried onions (store-bought)

2-3 green chillies, sliced in half lengthways

In a large bowl, combine the mince, soaked lentils, ginger, garlic, green chillies, ground spices, salt, yoghurt, biryani masala, coriander and mint leaves, lemon juice, tomatoes, and fried onions. Mix well.

Heat the vegetable oil in a large cooking pot and add the whole spices (cinnamon stick, cloves, and cardamon pods). Fry until fragrant, around 2 minutes, then add the mince and lentil mixture. Mix well to combine.

Cook for 6 to 7 minutes, stirring occasionally, then add 750ml of water and bring to boil. Cover and simmer on low heat for 30 minutes until the lentils have cooked through.

Garnish with the herbs, a sprinkling of fried onions, and the green chillies. Serve hot with rice, parathas, or naan.

SABUT MASOOR DAAL WITH SPINACH (SPICED BROWN LENTILS WITH SPINACH)

India

Prep time: 10 minutes | Cooking time: 1 hour (40 minutes, if using a pressure cooker) | Serves 4

These spiced brown lentils, known as Sabut Masoor Daal in India, make a hearty and nutritious dish that serves as a staple in many Indian households. This comforting meal is made by simmering whole brown lentils until tender and then cooking them in a flavourful blend of onions, tomatoes, garlic, ginger, and aromatic spices like cumin, coriander, and turmeric. The result is a rich, creamy daal with a slightly earthy flavour.

I have prepared this Sabut Masoor Daal with spinach to enhance its flavour and nutritional value and make it a complete one-pot meal. This daal is my go-to comfort food, and it's best enjoyed with hot rice and a side of pickle.

200g dried brown lentils, washed and soaked in water for 1 to 2 hours

2 tsp turmeric powder

Salt, to taste

1-1.25L water

2 tbsp ghee or vegetable oil

1 medium onion, finely chopped

1 tsp garlic paste

1 tsp ginger paste

½ tin of chopped tomatoes (200g)

1 tbsp tomato purée

1 tsp ground coriander

½ tsp ground cumin

250g spinach leaves, roughly chopped

1 tsp garam masala

1 lemon, juiced

1 handful of fresh coriander leaves, chopped, to garnish

Add the drained lentils, 1 teaspoon of turmeric, a pinch of salt, and one litre of water to a pan and bring to a boil for 20 to 25 minutes until tender and cooked. If using a pressure cooker, add the drained lentils, turmeric, salt, and 750ml of water and cook for 10 to 12 minutes.

In a separate pan, heat the ghee or oil, and sauté the chopped onions for 10 minutes until golden brown. Add the ginger and garlic paste and cook on a medium heat for 5 minutes.

Add the chopped tomatoes and tomato purée, mix well, then cover and cook for 6 to 7 minutes, stirring occasionally. Add 250ml of water if you find the mixture is too thick or is sticking to the base of the pan.

Add the ground coriander, cumin, remaining turmeric, a pinch of salt, and chopped spinach and stir well. Turn to a low heat and cook for 10 minutes until the spinach wilts.

Pour the cooked lentils into the spiced spinach and mix well. Add the garam masala, then finish with a squeeze of lemon juice and garnish with coriander leaves. Serve hot with rice, rotis or bread.

EGGS

AN EGG-CEPTIONAL TRIO
KOREA, MYANMAR, AND INDIA

India, Myanmar (formerly Burma), and Korea share deep cultural connections that span history, language, and religion. From the shared influences of Buddhism to the migration of spices and cooking methods, the culinary landscapes of India, Myanmar, and Korea are a testament to the enduring impact of cultural exchange.

India and Korea have a long history of trade relations dating back to ancient times. The Maritime Silk Road, which connected Asia with the rest of the world, played a key role in facilitating trade and cultural exchange between India and Korea. Additionally, Korean cuisine has been significantly influenced by its Buddhist roots, as seen in the prominence of vegetarian dishes in temple food, and this stems from the introduction of Buddhism from India and its philosophy of ahimsa (non-violence).

Indian and Korean cuisines are both known for their bold and robust flavours. Both Indian and Korean cuisines have a rich tradition of fermented foods, which are integral to their culinary practices. In Korea, fermented foods like kimchi and gochujang are staples, while in India, pickles and fermented lentil and rice batters, used in dishes like dosa and dhokla, play a similar role. **Gochujang Eggs** is a popular dish in Korean cuisine that typically involves soft-boiled or hard-boiled eggs served with a spicy and savoury gochujang-based sauce. There is a growing trend of culinary fusion between the two cuisines, especially in global cities with diverse populations. Dishes like 'Korean-style curry' or 'Indian kimchi' reflect this blend. Korean curry, for instance, has been adapted with more Indian-style spices, while Indian dishes may incorporate gochujang for a Korean twist.

Besides the ancient, deep-rooted connections forged through Buddhism and trade, the cultural exchange between India and Myanmar was further strengthened during the British colonial period when many Indians migrated to Myanmar (then Burma) for work. British rule facilitated the movement of Indians to Burma, leading to the establishment of a strong Indian diaspora there. This migration contributed to a vibrant cultural exchange, with Indians bringing their traditions, cuisine, and practices to Burma. Burmese cuisine has been heavily influenced by Indian culinary traditions and is often described as a blend of Indian, Chinese, and Thai influences. This fusion is evident in dishes like **Egg Bhejo** and Atho Noodles (see page 110). Both Indian and Burmese cuisines feature richly spiced dishes with various curry preparations, using common spices such as turmeric, cumin, coriander, and chilli, reflecting their shared culinary heritage.

The **Malabar Omelette Curry** recipe in this section is inspired by Moplah cuisine, also known as Mappila cuisine, which is the traditional cuisine of the Muslim community in the Malabar region of Kerala, India. Moplah cuisine is heavily influenced by the Arab traders who came to the Malabar coast centuries ago in search of spices and is characterised by its generous use of spices like black pepper, cardamom, cloves, and other aromatic spices. These traders left a lasting impact on the culinary practices of the region, blending local ingredients with Arabic and Persian cooking techniques.

With their aromatic spices, chilli heat, and rich flavours, it's egg-citing to see the similarities and differences between these cuisines expressed through one of the world's most simple and versatile ingredients: the humble egg.

GOCHUJANG EGGS

Korea

Prep time: 20 minutes | Cooking time: 15 minutes (25 minutes if the eggs aren't pre-boiled) | Serves 4

Gochujang Eggs is a simple and flavourful recipe that combines the richness of eggs with the bold flavours of Korean gochujang paste. The blend of spicy gochujang, aromatic garlic, and creamy butter creates a delicious sauce that perfectly complements the hard-boiled eggs.

This dish has become a popular brunch staple in my home due to its unique flavour profile and how easy it is to prepare. It's such a delicious way start the day. Whether served on crusty sourdough bread or with a side of steamed rice, it always offers a delightful balance of spicy, savoury, and umami flavours.

2 tbsp butter

4-5 cloves of garlic, finely chopped

2 tbsp gochujang paste, mixed with 1 tbsp water

1 tbsp light soy sauce

1 tsp rice vinegar

250ml water

2 spring onions, chopped

1 tsp white and black sesame seeds, toasted

4 eggs, hard-boiled and sliced in half

1 tbsp chives, chopped, to garnish

Heat the butter in a pan and sauté the garlic for a minute. Combine the gochujang, soy sauce and vinegar to make a paste, then add to the pan and cook for 30 seconds.

Add the water to make a thick sauce, then sprinkle over the spring onions and sesame seeds and mix well. Place the eggs in the pan, cover, and leave to cook on a low heat for 4 to 5 minutes.

Check for seasoning, garnish with chopped chives, and serve over rice or toast.

BURMESE EGG BHEJO

Myanmar

Prep time: 30 minutes | Cooking time: 10 minutes (if you haven't pre-boiled the eggs) | Serves 4

Egg Bhejo is a popular Burmese street food dish consisting of boiled eggs stuffed with a tangy and spicy filling. Often served with a garnish of fresh coriander leaves, this egg dish can be enjoyed on its own as a snack, but it's also eaten with a spicy noodle dish called Atho (see page 110).

Egg Bhejo fascinates me because of how it illustrates the close culinary connection between Myanmar (Burma) and India. This tangy, spicy dish blends classic Indian flavours of fried onion, garlic, and peanut powder, with more traditional Burmese ingredients like lemon, tamarind, and salt water. Salt water, though a simple seasoning method, is a hallmark of Burmese cuisine and is commonly used to enhance the flavour of dishes, like salads and soups.

Neutral oil, for frying

2 medium onions, thinly sliced

10-12 cloves of garlic, sliced

3 tbsp unsalted peanuts, roasted and coarsely pounded

4 large eggs, hard-boiled, shells removed

FOR THE TOPPING

2 tbsp tamarind juice (soak 1 golf ball-sized piece in warm water for 15 minutes, then mash the tamarind in the water. Strain the liquid.)

1 tbsp lemon juice

1 tbsp salt water (1 tbsp water with ¼ tsp salt)

1 tbsp vegetable oil

2 tsp red chilli flakes

1 handful of coriander leaves, chopped, to garnish

Heat some oil in a pan and fry the onions until golden brown. Remove from the pan and set aside, then fry the garlic in the same pan until crispy. Set aside with the onion.

Dry roast the peanuts in a pan for 2 to 3 minutes, then coarsely grind in a pestle and mortar or add to a blender and pulse a few times. Set aside.

Put the tamarind juice, lemon juice, and salt water in three separate small bowls.

To stuff the eggs, create a slit down the centre of each egg, lengthways, but don't cut them completely in half.

Carefully stuff a small spoonful of the fried onion and garlic into each egg, along with some crushed peanuts.

Drizzle half a teaspoon each of tamarind and lemon juice over the stuffed egg, as well as a little salt water.

Heat 1 tablespoon of vegetable oil in a hot pan with the red chilli flakes. When hot, top each egg with the chilli oil and sprinkle with more fried onions and some chopped coriander before serving.

MALABAR OMELETTE CURRY

India

Prep time: 20 minutes | Cooking time: 40 minutes | Serves 4

This omelette curry is a delightful dish from the Malabar coast of India. The omelette pieces are immersed in a rich curry base made with onions, tomatoes, ginger, and garlic, simmered with a blend of spices and enriched with coconut milk. The omelette strips absorb the curry flavours, making this a hearty and flavourful dish. This dish can be served with rice, flatbreads, or slices of chunky bread to mop up the delicious gravy.

I discovered this dish during my travels around Kerala and loved the combination. I often prepare it with or without coconut milk, depending on my mood and the ingredients I have on hand. The gravy for this dish is thick and should wrap around the omelette strips.

FOR THE SPICE PASTE

½ tsp cumin seeds

½ tsp fennel seeds

2 tsp ground coriander

½ tsp chilli powder

½ tsp garam masala

½ tsp turmeric

3 tbsp water

FOR THE OMELETTE

4 large eggs, beaten

I small onion, finely chopped

2 green chillies, finely chopped

I tbsp coriander leaves, chopped

Salt and pepper, to taste

FOR THE GRAVY

2-3 tbsp vegetable or coconut oil

2 medium onions, finely sliced

I tsp ginger paste

I tsp garlic paste

100ml water, if required

½ tin of chopped tomatoes (200g)

2-3 green chillies, finely chopped

200ml coconut milk

I tsp malt vinegar

I tbsp coriander leaves, chopped, to garnish

Salt, to taste

To make the spice paste, put all the spices into a blender and blitz to a fine powder. Stir in 3 tablespoons of water and set aside.

To make the omelette, combine the ingredients and mix well. Heat a little vegetable oil in a frying pan and pour in the egg mix. When cooked underneath, flip the omelette with a large spatula and cook the other side through, about 3 to 4 minutes. Remove from the heat and set aside to cool.

To make the gravy, heat the vegetable or coconut oil in a large pan and add the sliced onions. Sauté over medium heat for 10 to 12 minutes. Add the ginger and garlic pastes and cook for a further 5 minutes.

Add the spice paste and cook for 3 to 4 minutes – you can also add a little more water if the mixture starts to stick to the pan. Add the tomatoes, green chillies, and sauté for a further 5 minutes. Next, add the coconut milk, mix well, and simmer for 10 minutes.

Cut the omelette into wide strips then add them to the pan along with the vinegar and coriander leaves. Cook on a low heat for 3 to 4 minutes, then season to taste with salt. Serve with rice, bread or rotis.

POTATOES

THE PATATA PATH

SPAIN, INDIA, AND LEBANON

The similarity between the words for potatoes in India, Spain, and Lebanon – 'patata' and 'batata' – really caught my interest. I started wondering how these different places could share the same word, and that curiosity led me to explore the culinary links between them.

The term 'patata' comes from the Spanish for potato, derived from a blend of the Taino word 'batata' (sweet potato) and the Quechua word 'papa' (potato). Spanish explorers introduced potatoes to Europe from the Americas in the 16th century, and the term spread to various languages due to trade, cultural exchanges, and colonial influence. In Lebanese Arabic, 'batata' is used for potatoes, while in some Indian languages, the term has been borrowed due to the historical Portuguese presence.

The spice trade was a major influence in shaping the culinary landscape of Southern Spain, and the ingredients and produce brought over from India and the Middle East have contributed to the rich and diverse flavours that characterise the region's cuisine today. This influence can be traced back to the period of Arab and Moorish rule in Spain (711-1492), during which new agricultural practices, culinary techniques, and ingredients were introduced, such as rice, sugar, almonds, saffron and black pepper. These ingredients, sourced from India and Southeast Asia, became integral to Spanish cooking and are essential to many traditional dishes today. The lingering influence of the Moors' rustic cooking style, such as slow-cooking vegetables in olive oil, is also evident in many Andalusian recipes, such as **Patatas a lo Pobre** ('Poor Man's Potatoes').

Potatoes were introduced to India by Portuguese traders in the early 17th century. The Portuguese, having established colonies in Goa and other parts of India, brought many crops from the New World, including potatoes. Potatoes quickly became a staple in Indian cuisine due to their versatility and ability to absorb the rich spices and flavours characteristic of Indian cooking. Classic examples include Dum Aloo, **Tandoori Aloo**, and Aloo Paratha (with "aloo" being the Hindi word for potato.)

Potatoes were introduced to Lebanon and the broader Levant region during the late 18th or early 19th century, likely through trade routes and the gradual integration of the crop into the local agricultural system. The exact timeline of the introduction is not well-documented, but it is believed that potatoes were brought to Lebanon from South America via European traders and subsequently adapted to local growing conditions. Potatoes have become a staple ingredient in the country's cuisine, appearing in various traditional dishes, such as **Batata Harra** (spicy potatoes), Batata wa Bayd (potatoes and eggs), and Kibbeh Bi-batata (potato kibbeh), among others.

Experience the wonderful adaptability of this humble root vegetable in this trio of dishes from Spain, India, and Lebanon!

PATATAS
A LO POBRE
Spain

Prep time: 15 minutes | Cooking time: 50 minutes | Serves 4

Patatas a lo Pobre is a traditional Spanish dish that translates to 'Poor Man's Potatoes'. It is a simple and rustic dish made with potatoes, onions, peppers, and garlic cooked in olive oil.

I first tasted this dish during my visits to Granada and Seville in southern Spain, and I instantly fell in love with its flavours. The combination of tender potatoes, slow cooked onions, and savoury peppers left a real impression on my palate.

This dish can be seen as a blend of Spanish and Moorish cuisine. The Moors, who ruled large parts of Spain from the 8th to the 15th centuries, left a significant cultural and culinary legacy. The proximity of southern Spain to North Africa resulted in the culinary exchange of flavours and culinary practices, which is reflected here in this dish's rustic cooking style and basic ingredients, with the use of smoked paprika bringing a distinctly Spanish touch.

10 tbsp olive oil

3 large onions, thinly sliced

Salt, to taste

2-3 bay leaves

6-8 cloves of garlic, thinly sliced

3 peppers, deseeded and roughly chopped (green and red)

800g medium potatoes, cut into thick slices

1 tsp smoked paprika

20g fresh parsley, finely chopped

Heat half the olive oil in a pan, then add the onions and a pinch of salt and cook slowly for about 20 minutes, stirring occasionally, until the onions are golden-brown.

Add the bay leaves, garlic, and peppers and cook on a low-medium heat for 10 minutes. Add the remaining oil to the pan once the peppers have softened, then add the sliced potato and paprika. Season with salt and mix well.

Let the potatoes fry gently for 15 minutes or until tender, then remove the excess oil by draining the potatoes and peppers in a colander. You can reserve the excess oil and use it next time you cook.

Check for seasoning and garnish with chopped parsley. Serve hot as a side dish with roast chicken or lamb or enjoy on its own with some crusty bread.

TANDOORI ALOO

India

Prep time: 10 minutes | Cooking time: 45 minutes | Serves 4-6

This humble potato dish is a flavour bomb and an all-time crowd pleaser! Not only that, it's also super easy to make. This dish is like roast potatoes but with an added oomph of delicious tandoori flavours.

In this simple recipe, potatoes are tossed in an aromatic spice blend called tandoori masala and then cooked in the oven. 'Masala' refers to a blend of spices used in Indian cuisine, and tandoori masala is made with spices such as cumin, coriander, ginger, garlic powder, paprika, mango powder, cardamom and sometimes fenugreek, cloves, and cinnamon.

Once cooked, the potatoes turn a deep red colour, and this dish is one of my favourites – it is always a hit! I served it as one of my supper club courses on Channel 4's Double the Money. Enjoy this tasty starter with your favourite garnishes or as a delightful side dish with any meal.

7-8 tbsp vegetable oil

1 tsp cumin seeds

3 tbsp tandoori masala

Salt, to taste

800g potatoes, cubed

1 lemon, juiced, to serve

1 red onion, thinly sliced, to garnish

15g fresh coriander leaves, chopped, to garnish

Preheat the oven to 200°c, then heat the oil in large wok. Add the cumin seeds, tandoori masala, and salt, and fry until fragrant. Add the potatoes, mix well, then transfer the masala potatoes into a baking dish.

Bake the potatoes in the oven for 30 to 40 minutes or until cooked through. Serve with a squeeze of lemon, sliced red onion, and chopped coriander leaves.

BATATA HARRA

Lebanon

Prep time: 10 minutes | Cooking time: 30 minutes | Serves 4

Batata Harra, translating to 'Spicy Potatoes', is a popular Middle Eastern dish, particularly in Lebanese cuisine. The dish is made with cubed potatoes that are typically fried until crispy and then tossed with a flavourful mixture of garlic, chilli peppers, and fresh herbs.

I absolutely love wrapping my crispy Batata Harra in a warm flatbread with some fresh salad, a generous drizzle of creamy tahini sauce, and a sprinkle of hot chilli peppers. The combination of flavours and textures creates a delightful party in your mouth with every bite.

This versatile dish can be served as a side dish, appetiser, or as part of a mezze.

Neutral oil, to deep fry
800g medium potatoes, peeled and cubed
2 tsp garlic, minced
1 red pepper, finely chopped
1 tsp paprika
1 tsp red chilli flakes

Salt and pepper, to taste
1 lemon, juiced
2 tbsp fresh coriander, chopped
2 tbsp fresh parsley, chopped

Warm the oil in a deep pan until very hot, then deep fry the potatoes until golden brown and crispy. Drain and set aside.

Heat 2 tablespoons of oil in a separate pan and sauté the garlic and red pepper for 2 to 4 minutes. Add the paprika, chilli flakes, salt, pepper, and fried potatoes, then toss well to combine.

Remove from the heat and finish with a drizzle of lemon juice and a sprinkling of fresh herbs. Serve hot by itself or with flatbreads and a side salad.

BEETROOT

BEETROOT BRIDGES
INDIA, GREECE, AND THE MIDDLE EAST

The Hellenistic period (323-31 BCE) followed Alexander the Great's conquests and saw the spread of Greek culture across a vast empire, stretching from the Mediterranean to Central Asia. During this era, there was a significant exchange of ingredients and cooking techniques which saw the blending of Greek, Persian, Egyptian, and other regional cuisines. This has had a lasting impact and contributed to a diverse culinary heritage that continues to evolve to this day.

Beetroot is a popular ingredient across India, Greece, and the Middle East. They are believed to have originated in the Mediterranean region and were cultivated and consumed by ancient civilisations such as the Greeks and Romans. The exchange of culinary ideas and ingredients between these regions during the Hellenistic period contributed to the spread of beetroot-based dishes and their integration into local cuisines.

In India, beetroot is used in savoury curries, salads, and desserts like halwa; Greek cuisine features beetroot in salads and mezze dishes; while in the Middle East, beetroot is used in salads, dips, and pickled or cooked as a side dish. The versatile use of beetroot, which adds colour, flavour, and nutritional value to a variety of dishes, highlights its adaptability and universal appeal in diverse culinary contexts.

Across **Beetroot Poriyal**, **Patzarosalata** and **Salat al Shamander**, I demonstrate how a single ingredient, like beetroot, has evolved to suit local flavours and techniques. I invite you to discover the versatility of this bold root vegetable and appreciate how it has been creatively adapted and celebrated across these Indian, Greek, and Middle Eastern dishes.

BEETROOT PORIYAL

India

Prep time: 10 minutes | Cooking time: 20 minutes | Serves 4

Beetroot Poriyal is a South Indian stir fry dish of chopped beetroot sautéed with mustard seeds, curry leaves and coconut. It's the South Indian equivalent of a quick, dry stir fry.

The key features of poriyal are that it can be made with a variety of vegetables. The vegetables are typically cooked to retain their crunchy texture, and it is not heavily spiced, allowing the natural taste of the vegetables to shine through.

This mildly spiced beetroot dish is an easy recipe, and it's perfect as a side dish with rice and lentils or enjoyed as a warm salad.

2 tbsp coconut or neutral oil

1 tsp urad dal (split black lentils), soaked in 2 tbsp water for 20 minutes and rinsed

1 tsp black mustard seeds

10-12 curry leaves

1 tsp ginger, grated

4 medium-sized raw beetroots, peeled and chopped

2 green chillies, halved

Salt, to taste

2 tbsp desiccated coconut

A handful of fresh coriander leaves, chopped

Heat the oil in a pan, then add the soaked and rinsed urad dal and mustard seeds. Let them crackle for a few seconds. Add the curry leaves and ginger and sauté for a few seconds until fragrant.

Add the chopped beetroot and mix well, then add the green chillies and a pinch of salt to taste. Mix everything together.

Cover the pan with a lid and cook the beetroot on a low-medium heat, stirring occasionally, until the beetroot is tender. This will take about 8 to 10 minutes. Once the beetroot is cooked, add the desiccated coconut and mix well.

Garnish with chopped coriander leaves and serve immediately to enjoy the beetroot poriyal's fresh flavours and crunchy texture.

PATZAROSALATA (ROAST BEETROOT SALAD)
Greece

Prep time: 10 minutes | Cooking time: 45 minutes, if roasting; 30 minutes, if boiling | Serves 4

Patzarosalata is a classic Greek salad made with roasted or boiled beets tossed in a tangy dressing with feta, pistachios, garlic, and herbs.

The combination of earthy beets, tangy vinaigrette, and creamy feta creates a delicious and nutritious side dish or vegetarian main course. The name 'patzarosalata' comes from the Greek word 'pantzári', meaning beetroot, and 'saláta', meaning salad. This dish is a staple of Greek cuisine and is often served as part of a mezze platter or alongside other traditional Greek dishes.

4 medium-sized raw beetroots
1 small red onion, thinly sliced
2 cloves of garlic, finely chopped
A handful of fresh parsley, chopped
A handful of fresh dill
1 lemon, juiced
3 tbsp olive oil
25g shelled pistachios, coarsely chopped
100g feta cheese

Roast the beetroots in a preheated oven at 200°c for about 40 to 45 minutes until tender. Let the cooked beetroots cool slightly, then peel off the skin and cut into cubes. You can also boil the beetroots instead of roasting them, which reduces the cooking time significantly. Simply peel and dice the beetroots, then boil them in water for about 20 to 30 minutes until tender. Allow the boiled beetroots to cool before using them in the salad as directed.

In a large mixing bowl, combine the cubed beetroot, sliced red onion, garlic, herbs, and lemon juice. Drizzle over the olive oil and season to taste. Add the pistachios and crumbled feta then gently toss to evenly coat the salad. Serve at room temperature or chilled, depending on your preference.

NOTE

While yoghurt is common in Greek cuisine, particularly in dishes like tzatziki, it's not typically found in patzarosalata. Instead, this salad gets its creamy texture from the crumbled feta cheese, which adds a salty, tangy flavour. Some variations may include a dollop of Greek yoghurt as a garnish, but it's not considered traditional.

SALAT AL-SHAMANDAR

Middle East

Prep time: 15 minutes | Cooking time: 45 minutes | Serves 4-6

Salat al-Shamandar is a Middle Eastern beetroot salad made with boiled or roasted beets, lemon juice, olive oil, salt, garlic, and herbs. Some variations also include tahini and yoghurt for added creaminess and flavour.

This dish is typically served as a side dish or appetiser, and is often enjoyed with bread, vegetables, or as part of a mezze platter. It is vibrant in colour, with tangy and earthy flavours, a refreshing taste, and its healthy qualities make it a popular choice in Middle Eastern countries, including Lebanon, Syria, and Jordan.

FOR THE SALAD

6 large raw beetroots, peeled and cut into 1-inch cubes

2 tbsp olive oil

Salt and pepper, to taste

25g walnuts, chopped

1 small red onion, thinly sliced

20g fresh parsley, chopped

20g fresh mint, chopped

FOR THE DRESSING

65g tahini

1 orange, juiced

2 tbsp olive oil

2 tbsp water

1 clove of garlic, minced

1 lemon, juiced

¼ tsp ground cumin

Preheat the oven to 200°c.

Toss the beetroot cubes with 2 tablespoons of olive oil and season with salt and pepper. Spread the beets out on a baking tray and roast for 30 minutes or until tender, making sure they're al dente and still have a little bite.

While the beetroot cools, whisk all the dressing ingredients together until smooth. Then, in a large bowl, toss the cooled, roasted beets with the walnuts and red onion before pouring the dressing over the salad. Toss well to coat, check for seasoning, and garnish with the chopped herbs.

This salad can be served immediately or refrigerated for a short time before serving (this will allow the flavours to meld and develop.)

MANGOES

A SHARED TROPICAL DELIGHT

INDIA, INDONESIA AND VIETNAM

The cultural and culinary tapestry of India, Indonesia, and Vietnam is intricately woven with threads of history, religion, and shared flavours. The Indian influence in these regions was primarily driven by the spread of Hinduism and Buddhism, which significantly shaped their cultural and religious landscapes.

In ancient times, the spread of these religions from India to Southeast Asia played a pivotal role in shaping the spiritual and cultural identities of Indonesia and Vietnam. For instance, the island of Bali in Indonesia predominantly follows Hinduism, which has deeply influenced local customs, rituals, and cuisine. In Vietnam, Buddhist practices have significantly influenced the cultural fabric of the land, leading to the development of a vegetarian cuisine that aligns with the religious principles of both Buddhism and Hinduism. Temples and religious festivals often feature dishes that reflect this rich heritage.

The culinary connections are just as profound. Indian cuisine has left a lasting impact on the flavours and cooking techniques used in Indonesian and Vietnamese cuisines. The use of spices such as turmeric, coriander, cumin, and cardamom in Indonesian dishes like Rendang and Soto can be traced back to Indian influences. Similarly, Vietnam's love for curries, such as Cà Ri Gà (chicken curry) and Cà Ri Chay (vegetable curry), demonstrates the Indian influence on their culinary traditions.

Mangoes, which originated in South Asia, serve as a delightful culinary bridge between India, Indonesia, and Vietnam. Through their shared love of this wondrous fruit, these nations continue to celebrate a legacy of interconnected traditions and flavours that highlight their shared heritage.

India, being one of the largest producers and consumers of mangoes, incorporates the fruit into a variety of dishes, both sweet and savoury. Mangoes hold a special place in the hearts (and stomachs) of India's people and are used in many ways, from refreshing drinks like Mango Lassi to tangy Mango Chuntney and creamy **Mango Shrikhand**. The latter, also known as Amrakhand, is a delightful dessert made by combining thick, strained yoghurt with ripe mango pulp.

In Indonesia, mangoes are cherished in dishes like Mango Sambal and **Rujak**, a fruit salad with a spicy twist. Meanwhile, Vietnamese cuisine incorporates mangoes in many dishes, such as refreshing salads, **Mango and Avocado Summer Rolls** (Gôi Cuôn Xoài), and desserts such as Che Chuoi and Mango Sticky Rice. The diversity of mangoes in Vietnam, such as Hoa Loc and Cat Chu, are celebrated for their sweet and aromatic qualities, making them a beloved ingredient in both traditional and modern recipes.

MADHU'S MANGO SHRIKHAND

India

Prep time: 1 hour 10 minutes, plus 1 hour chilling | Serves 4-6

Shrikhand is a popular Indian dessert made from strained yoghurt that's been sweetened with sugar and flavoured with spices like cardamom and saffron. This particular version is enhanced by the addition of sweet mangoes.

This dessert is loved for its rich, creamy texture, sweet and tangy flavour, and ease of preparation. With just a few simple ingredients, you can create a luxurious and indulgent dessert that's perfect for any occasion, whether a casual family gathering or a formal dinner party.

This is my younger sister Madhu's recipe. I always thought it was a complicated dish, but she really helped demystify the process and has shown me a quick way to make it.

500g Greek yoghurt or hung curd

250g mango pulp (fresh or tinned)

60g caster sugar

½ tsp ground cardamom

6-7 strands of saffron, soaked in 1 tbsp warm milk, plus more to garnish

100g fresh mango, chopped, to serve

1 tbsp pistachios nuts, chopped, to serve (or almonds)

Place the yoghurt in a muslin cloth and tie it up at the corners. Hang it over a bowl and let the excess water drain for at least an hour.

Mix the drained yoghurt, mango pulp, caster sugar, ground cardamom, and soaked saffron strands until well combined.

Garnish with addition saffron strands and chill in the refrigerator for at least 1 hour before serving.

Serve the chilled Mango Shrikhand in individual bowls or glasses. Garnish with fresh mango pieces, pistachios, and more saffron strands before serving.

MANGO RUJAK (MANGO SALAD)

Indonesia

Prep time: 25 minutes | Serves 4

Rujak, also known as Rojak, is a popular salad from Indonesia and Malaysia that combines a variety of fresh fruits and vegetables with a sweet and spicy sauce. The salad typically includes pineapple, cucumber, mango, jicama (a crunchy root vegetable), beansprouts, and tofu tossed together in a dressing of tamarind, palm sugar, shrimp paste, and chilli. Rujak is a refreshing and colourful dish that's perfect for hot weather or as a light lunch or snack. It is often garnished with fried shallots, nuts, and sambal for extra flavour and crunch.

I like to serve this Mango Rujak on a bed of rocket. Although it's not the traditional way, I think the rocket really enhances the flavour and texture of the salad.

FOR THE SALAD

2 ripe mangoes, peeled and cut in cubes

½ pineapple, peeled and cut into bite-sized pieces

1 cucumber, sliced thinly

2 green apples, sliced thinly

1 red onion, thinly sliced

3 tbsp roasted peanuts, chopped

100g rocket leaves

FOR THE DRESSING

2 tbsp tamarind paste

3 tbsp palm sugar (or brown sugar)

1 tbsp shrimp paste (optional)

2 red chillies, finely chopped (adjust to taste)

¼ tsp salt

1-2 tbsp water

TO GARNISH (OPTIONAL)

2 tbsp fried shallots

2 tbsp roasted peanuts, crushed

1 tbsp sambal

In a large bowl, combine the sliced fruit, onions, and chopped peanuts. Whisk the dressing ingredients together in a separate bowl until well combined, then pour the dressing over the fruit mixture and toss to coat evenly.

Let the salad sit for a few minutes to allow the flavours to meld and settle. Serve chilled on a bed of rocket leaves and enjoy.

MANGO AND AVOCADO SUMMER ROLLS

Vietnam

Prep time: 30 minutes | Serves 4 (8 rolls)

Vietnamese Summer Rolls, also known as Gôi Cuôn, are fresh and flavourful appetisers made by filling Vietnamese rice paper wrappers with a combination of meat, fish, vegetables, or fruit. Served cold with a sweet and savoury peanut dipping sauce, these make a refreshing option for a light meal or appetiser.

Gôi Cuôn is a popular dish in Vietnamese cuisine, known for its bright colours and fresh ingredients. These summer rolls are filled with ripe mango, creamy avocado, and crisp vegetables, and provide a delicious contrast of textures and flavours.

FOR THE PEANUT SAUCE

4 tbsp smooth peanut butter

250ml water (adjust as needed)

1 tbsp honey

1 lime, juiced

1 tsp soy sauce

2 tsp ginger, freshly grated

½ tsp red chilli flakes

FOR THE SUMMER ROLLS

8 6-inch Vietnamese rice paper wrappers

1 large handful of mixed fresh herbs, chopped (such as mint, coriander, and basil)

1 ripe avocado, peeled and thinly sliced

1 ripe mango, peeled and thinly sliced

1 small cucumber, julienned

8 lettuce leaves, torn into smaller pieces

To make the peanut sauce, add all the sauce ingredients to a blender and blend until smooth. If the mixture is too thick for dipping, add a small amount of water and blend again. Repeat until the desired consistency is reached.

To make the summer rolls, soak a rice paper wrapper in a shallow bowl filled with lukewarm water until pliable (about 10 seconds). Remove and lay flat on a clean surface. Add a few herbs to the centre of the wrapper followed by two to three slices of avocado. Next, add a few pieces each of the mango and cucumber slices, then top with just enough lettuce to still be able to close the wrapper.

Fold the sides of the wrapper inward, then fold the bottom up and begin to roll upwards. Close tightly and place the rolls seam side down on a plate. Repeat with the remaining ingredients to make eight rolls and serve chilled with the peanut sauce.

YOGHURT

A SPOONFUL OF HISTORY: HOW YOGHURT UNITES REGIONS
INDIA, NEPAL, AND THE MIDDLE EAST

Yoghurt is a versatile and nutritious ingredient that holds a special place in the culinary traditions of India, Nepal, and the Levant region. The culinary connections between these regions are rich and diverse, stemming from centuries of trade, migration, and historical interactions, which have left an indelible mark on their gastronomic landscapes.

The practice of fermenting milk to make yoghurt likely originated in the Middle East and spread to South Asia, including India and Nepal, through ancient migrations and trade. The Silk Road, for example, facilitated the movement of goods, ideas, and culinary practices between the East and the West. Yoghurt, with its health benefits and long shelf life, was a valuable commodity that spread along these routes.

In the Levant region of the Middle East, which includes countries like Lebanon, Syria, Jordan, and Israel, yoghurt is a central ingredient in many traditional dishes. Known locally as 'labneh' when strained, it offers a creamy, tangy flavour that enhances a wide array of recipes. Labneh, a thick, creamy yoghurt spread, can be enjoyed as a savoury dip or sweetened with honey and fruit for desserts. In addition, yoghurt-based sauces such as tzatziki, a cucumber and garlic yoghurt sauce, and jajik, a similar sauce with mint, are staples in Levantine cuisine.

In Indian cuisine, yoghurt, known as 'dahi', has been a staple for centuries. It is deeply embedded in the cultural and culinary practices, used in a variety of dishes from savoury to sweet, including the popular cooling side dish, raita. Its use can be traced back to ancient times and has been celebrated for its health benefits and versatility. It is even mentioned in the Vedas, the oldest texts of Hinduism. Another popular yoghurt-based item is lassi, which can either be made in a savoury version, with salt and spices, or a sweet version. Yoghurt is also commonly used as a marinade for meats and vegetables, tenderising them as well as adding a creamy texture to curries.

In Nepal, yoghurt is also referred to as 'dahi' and plays a crucial role in daily meals and festive or religious celebrations. In both Nepalese and Indian Hindu traditions, yoghurt is used in rituals such as pujas (prayer ceremonies) as well as being offered to deities. It is considered auspicious and is believed to have spiritual and physical benefits. This shared heritage has led to the widespread use of yoghurt across both cuisines, closely linking them through their religious practices.

The extensive use of yoghurt in India, Nepal, and the Levant highlights a history shared and shaped by ancient trade and cultural exchanges. Whether used in an Indian **Beetroot Raita**, a Nepalese **Aloo Chukauni**, or a creamy Levantine **Strawberry Labneh**, yoghurt continues to be a beloved and integral part of these cuisines, celebrating an enduring culinary connection.

BEETROOT RAITA

India

Prep time: 20 minutes | Cooking time: 10 minutes | Serves 4-6

Raita is a traditional Indian side dish made with yoghurt and a variety of chopped vegetables or fruits. It is typically seasoned with herbs and spices and is a cooling side dish that's often served alongside spicy curries to help balance out the flavours. There are many variations of raita, depending on regional preferences and the available ingredients.

Raitas can be served plain or with tempered spices for added flavour (like in this recipe). In Indian cooking, tempering is a technique used to enhance the flavour of a dish by infusing hot oil or ghee with various spices and aromatics.

I absolutely love the vibrant colour of beetroot raita, and it holds a special place in my heart as it was part of my winning thali in Amazon Prime's The World Cook. The beetroot not only adds a stunning hue but also brings a unique flavour to the creamy, tangy yoghurt base, making it a standout component of any meal.

3-4 tbsp water
2 large beetroots, peeled and grated
2-3 spring onions, finely chopped
2 green chillies, finely chopped
1 tsp ginger, grated
1 handful of coriander leaves, chopped
½ tsp ground cumin
Salt, to taste
300g Greek yoghurt, whisked

FOR THE TEMPERED SPICES (OPTIONAL)
1 tsp ghee or vegetable oil
1 tsp black mustard seeds
1-2 dried red chillies (optional)
6-7 curry leaves

Add 2 tablespoons of water to the grated beetroot and cook on a medium heat for 5 to 7 minutes. Alternatively, you can put them in a microwave for 3 to 4 minutes. Once tender, set aside to cool.

Add the cooled beetroot, chopped spring onion, green chillies, ginger, coriander leaves, cumin, and salt to the yoghurt and mix well to combine.

To temper the spices (optional), heat the oil in a small pan. Add the mustard seeds, dried chillies, and curry leaves till they splutter, then pour over the top of the yoghurt and serve.

ALOO CHUKAUNI
(POTATOES IN SESAME YOGHURT)

Nepal

Prep time: 25 minutes | Cooking time: 10 minutes | Serves 4

Aloo Chukauni is a traditional Nepalese dish made from boiled potatoes mixed with yoghurt, green chillies, roasted sesame seeds and a tempering of mustard seeds, turmeric, and garlic. This tangy and spicy salad is often enjoyed as a side dish or a refreshing accompaniment to main meals. I have added my 'radikal' twist to the recipe by incorporating mustard and dill.
I fell in love with this dish the first time I had it at my friend's place. I love the textures and taste, and I often enjoy it with a hot chapati and some pickle.

2 tbsp sesame seeds

500g Greek yoghurt, whisked

1 tsp chilli powder

1 tsp ground cumin

Salt, to taste

1 red onion, thinly sliced

1 green chilli, chopped

4-5 medium potatoes, boiled and cubed

1 tbsp lemon juice

1 tbsp fresh coriander leaves, chopped

10g fresh dill, chopped

½ tsp English mustard

1 tbsp mustard oil

½ tsp turmeric

1 tsp fenugreek seeds

Dry roast the sesame seeds in a small pan for 2 minutes until they are golden and fragrant. Allow to cool, then grind them to a fine powder using a processor or pestle and mortar.

Mix the yoghurt, chilli powder, ground sesame seeds, cumin and salt together in a bowl. Add the onion, green chilli, and boiled potatoes and mix well. Then, add the lemon juice, coriander leaves, dill, and English mustard, and stir to combine. Season to taste with salt and set aside.

Heat the mustard oil in a small pan, then add the turmeric and fenugreek seeds. Fry until fragrant, then drizzle the hot, seasoned oil over the yoghurt before serving.

LABNEH
WITH STRAWBERRIES
Middle East

Prep time: 4 hours 30 minutes | Serves 4-6

Labneh has roots in the Levant region, which includes Lebanon, Syria, Jordan, and Palestine. The beauty of labneh is that it can be enjoyed as either a sweet or savoury dish. It can be eaten as a dip, often garnished with olive oil, herbs, and spices for a savoury twist, or drizzled with honey and topped with fruits and nuts for a sweet treat. Labneh is my all-time favourite, and it is very easy to make at home.

Here's my special summer recipe of Labneh with Strawberries. It's the perfect treat for warm, sunny days.

1kg natural or full fat yoghurt

Salt, to taste

500g strawberries, plus extra to garnish

2 tsp caster sugar

2 tsp rose water

3 tbsp honey, plus extra to garnish

3 tbsp pistachios, chopped, to garnish

Edible rose petals, to garnish

To make the labneh, mix the yoghurt with a pinch of salt, then transfer to a muslin cloth and hang over a deep bowl to strain the excess liquid. Leave to drain in the fridge for approximately 4 hours.

Take a quarter of the strawberries and combine them with the sugar and rose water. Add to a blender and blitz to a purée. Chop the remaining strawberries and mix them with the puréed strawberries. Leave in the fridge until the chopped strawberries have softened.

After it has been strained for 4 hours, remove the labneh (or hung curd) from the muslin cloth, add the honey, and fold the strawberries through.

Garnish the strawberry labneh with more sliced strawberries, crushed pistachios, a drizzle of honey and edible rose petals before serving chilled.

MILK
CREAMY CONNECTIONS
SPAIN, INDIA, AND BANGLADESH

Who doesn't love milk-based desserts? They are a firm favourite in my family, cherished for their rich and creamy textures. As we explore these delightful treats, we uncover deep cultural significance and traditions in South Asia and Spain.

In South Asia, particularly in India, Bangladesh and Pakistan, milk-based puddings like kheer (payesh in Bengali) and **Shemai** hold a special place in festive celebrations and rituals. Kheer, made by simmering rice in milk with sugar, cardamom, and sometimes saffron, symbolises prosperity and good fortune. Often served as a blessed offering to deities, kheer is shared among family and friends during joyous occasions such as Diwali, Eid, and weddings. Seviyan, Semian, or vermicelli pudding, is another cherished dessert popular during Eid. The practice of preparing and sharing Seviyan during Eid al-Fitr beautifully captures the essence of community and togetherness.

In Spain, **Arroz con Leche** (rice pudding) has a history dating back to the Middle Ages. This Spanish delicacy typically consists of short-grain rice, milk, sugar, cinnamon, and citrus peel. Arroz con Leche is an essential part of Spanish culinary heritage, often served during special occasions like Christmas. Its origins trace back to the Moorish occupation of the Iberian Peninsula from the 8th to the 15th centuries, when the Moors introduced rice and various culinary traditions, including the use of milk and sugar in desserts.

My love for kheer, or payesh, and Arroz con Leche transcends borders and holds a special place in my heart due to the personal connections they evoke. **Paneer Payesh** stirs cherished memories of family gatherings and vibrant festivities. Each spoonful transports me back to joyous moments shared with loved ones.

On the other hand, Arroz con Leche connects me to my husband's German and Spanish lineage. As I savour this delightful dish, I am reminded of the warm, intimate family celebrations that have become an integral part of our shared life. Arroz con Leche represents the blending of our cultural backgrounds and the emotional bond we share through food, traditions, and love. Together, these two milk-based puddings not only showcase the global appeal of sweet delights but also symbolize the profound role that food plays in forging deep personal connections, whether that's during religious and cultural holidays, or simply served at my own family's dinner table.

MARINA'S ARROZ CON LECHE (RICE PUDDING)

Spain

Prep time: 10 minutes | Cooking time: 1 hour | Serves 4-6

Arroz con Leche, translating to 'rice with milk', is a creamy and indulgent rice pudding popular in many Spanish-speaking countries, including Mexico, Spain, and countries across Central and South America. It is made by cooking rice with milk, sugar, and cinnamon until the rice becomes soft and creamy, forming a thick pudding. The dish can be served warm or cold and is often topped with a sprinkling of ground cinnamon.

This recipe is from my mother-in-law, Marina, who lives in Barcelona. We have enjoyed her delicious rice pudding during special occasions, and it always brings a sense of warmth and joy. It reminds me of my own Indian culture, where rice pudding is also a cherished dessert served during festive moments. Sharing Marina's recipe brings back fond memories of family gatherings and the beautiful relationship between our culinary traditions.

1 L whole milk
1-inch cinnamon stick
Pinch of salt, to taste
60g short-grain white rice (like arborio)
60g caster sugar
1 tsp ground cinnamon

In a medium saucepan, combine the milk, cinnamon stick, and salt. Bring to the boil and stir frequently.

Add the rice, reduce to a simmer, then cover and leave to cook for 30 to 35 minutes, stirring occasionally, until the rice is soft and tender. Add the sugar, then cover and cook on a low heat for another 15 minutes. The texture should now be thick and creamy.

Remove from the heat and allow the rice pudding to cool. Sprinkle with ground cinnamon and serve warm or chilled.

MA'S PANEER PAYESH

India

Prep time: 10 minutes | Cooking time: 35 minutes | Serves 4-6

Paneer Payesh, also known as Chennar Payesh or Paneer Kheer, is a rich and creamy Bengali dessert, a little like rice pudding. Payesh, or kheer, holds a significant place in Indian culture, both as a sweet dessert and as a symbol of auspiciousness. It is often served during festivals, weddings, and other special occasions, as it is considered to bring good luck, prosperity, and happiness. This recipe has a special place in my heart, as it is one of my mother's signature dishes. She uses condensed milk instead of sugar, lending a rich sweetness to the dish that sets it apart from other recipes. Each year, my mother makes Paneer Payesh to celebrate our birthdays, making it an endearing tradition that I deeply cherish.

1L whole milk
200g paneer, cut into small cubes
4 tbsp condensed milk
¼ tsp ground cardamom
75g nuts, chopped, to garnish (like almonds or pistachios)

Boil the milk in a heavy-bottomed pan and reduce it by half. Keep stirring at regular intervals to prevent it from burning or catching on the bottom of the pan.

Once the milk becomes a thick and creamy consistency, add the chopped paneer and cook for another 5 to 6 minutes on a low heat.

Add the condensed milk and ground cardamom and mix well. Cover with a lid and remove from the heat. Set aside to cool, then refrigerate the payesh and serve chilled with a sprinkling of chopped nuts.

SHEMAI (VERMICELLI MILK PUDDING)

Bangladesh

Prep time: 10 minutes | Cooking time: 30 minutes | Serves 4-6

Shemai is a traditional dessert in Bangladesh and West Bengal, India, made with roasted vermicelli noodles, spiced milk, and sugar. It's often garnished with nuts and has a unique flavour and aroma from spices like saffron, bay leaf, cinnamon, cardamom, and star anise. Shemai is particularly special in Bangladeshi culture because it's a popular item during both Hindu and Islamic festivals, such as Eid, but it is also enjoyed throughout the year at family gatherings and special occasions.

Shemai, or Semai, is the Bengali word for vermicelli. The pudding is typically served at room temperature, although it can also be enjoyed chilled, depending on personal preference.

2 tbsp ghee

40g vermicelli noodles (shemai)

1L whole milk

30g sugar, or 4 tbsp condensed milk

¼ tsp ground cardamom

2 tbsp nuts, chopped (like almonds, cashews, or pistachios)

Heat the ghee in a pan over a medium heat. Toast the vermicelli noodles in the ghee until they turn golden-brown (about 3 to 5 minutes), making sure to stir continuously to prevent them from burning. Remove the toasted vermicelli from the pan and set aside.

Add the milk to a saucepan and bring to the boil. Reduce to a simmer and cook for 15 minutes until the milk reduces slightly, stirring occasionally to prevent it from sticking to the bottom. Add the roasted vermicelli and cook for about 10 to 15 minutes until softened and the mixture has reduced.

Add the sugar or condensed milk and cook on a low heat for another 5 minutes, then stir in the ground cardamom. Garnish with chopped nuts and serve at room temperature or chilled.

CUCUMBER

COOL AS A CUCUMBER

INDIA, IRAN, AND SPAIN

Cucumber is widely used in salads around the world for its crunchy texture and cooling properties, making it a refreshing addition to various dishes, especially in warm climates.

In India, cucumber salad, known as **Kachumber** is a simple yet refreshing dish that serves as a cooling side in the country's hotter regions. This salad typically includes diced cucumber, tomatoes, onions, and a splash of lemon juice, and it's often spiced with chilli and cumin. Its appeal is universal, and it has found its way into various cuisines around the world, with unique local adaptations.

In Spain's Andalusian region, there is a similar dish known as **Pipirrana Salad**, or 'Ensalada de Pipirrana' in Spanish. Including finely chopped cucumber, green peppers, tomatoes, and onions dressed with olive oil and vinegar, this salad makes a refreshing side dish for the rich, hearty flavours typical of Spanish cuisine. The addition of green peppers and the use of olive oil and vinegar reflects the country's Mediterranean influences and the abundance of these ingredients in the region.

In Iran, a comparable salad, known as **Salad Shirazi** (or Sālād-é-Shirāzi), uses cucumber, tomatoes, onions, and a dressing of lime juice or vinegar and fresh herbs like mint or parsley. This salad is a staple in Persian cuisine, offering a bright, cooling contrast to the more robust, spiced dishes it often accompanies. Named after the city of Shiraz, this salad is the perfect partner to Iran's hot summer months.

Despite their differences, these variations of cucumber salad share the same fundamental appeal: they're light, refreshing, and cooling, making them a must-have dish in their sun-drenched countries of origin. Each region has integrated local ingredients and flavours to make these their own, resulting in salads that are similar yet distinct, reflecting the unique yet comfortingly familiar culinary traditions of each culture.

KACHUMBER SALAD (CHOPPED CUCUMBER SALAD)

India

Prep time: 15 minutes | Serves 4

Kachumber is a traditional Indian salad made with freshly chopped cucumbers, tomatoes, onions, and green chillies. This is one of the most well-known salads in Indian cuisine, and it is also one of the easiest dishes to put together. Kachumber is also customisable, with variations adding different vegetables, herbs, and spices. It can be made spicy or mild, depending on personal preference.

In Indian cuisine, salads are traditionally served as accompaniments or side dishes within a larger meal. Unlike Western salads, Indian salads typically do not include oil in their dressings and are seasoned with minimal ingredients. This salad is dressed with lime juice and spices, giving it a refreshing and tangy flavour.

1 cucumber, chopped

2 medium tomatoes, chopped

1 red onion finely chopped

1 green chilli, finely chopped (optional)

Salt and pepper, to taste

Pinch of sugar, to taste

1 lemon or lime, juiced

30g fresh coriander, chopped

Mix the chopped cucumber, tomatoes, onions, and chilli in a large bowl. Season with salt, pepper, and sugar, then dress with the lime or lemon juice. Serve immediately, garnished with chopped coriander leaves.

NOTE

You could also add pomegranate seeds, raw mango, and carrots, as well as various herbs to customise your salad.

SHIRAZI SALAD

Iran

Prep time: 20 minutes | Serves 4

Shirazi Salad, or Sālād-é-Shirāzi, is a traditional Persian salad from the city of Shiraz in southern Iran. It's a refreshing and simple side dish that combines diced cucumbers, tomatoes, onions, and fresh herbs like mint and coriander. Though often dressed with a mixture of lemon or lime juice, salt, and pepper, the traditional dressing uses ab-ghooreh, a sour grape juice that can be hard to find outside of Iran.

Shirazi Salad is often served as a side dish, providing a refreshing complement to any meal.

FOR THE SALAD

1 cucumber, or 3 Persian cucumbers, diced

4 large vine tomatoes, diced

1 red onion, diced

200g pomegranate seeds

15g fresh mint leaves, chopped

10g fresh parsley leaves, chopped

10g fresh coriander leaves, chopped

FOR THE DRESSING

5 tbsp extra-virgin olive oil

2 limes, juiced

1 tsp sumac

Salt and pepper, to taste

Add the diced cucumber, tomato, and onion to a large salad bowl and combine. Add the pomegranate seeds and chopped herbs, stir to combine, then store in the fridge until ready to serve.

To make the dressing, combine the olive oil, lime juice, sumac, salt, and pepper. Mix well until emulsified and slightly thickened. When ready to serve, add the sumac dressing to the salad and toss everything until well coated.

PIPIRRANA SUMMER SALAD

Spain

Prep time: 15 minutes, plus 30 minutes chilling | Cooking time: 10 minutes | Serves 4

Pipirrana is a traditional Spanish salad from the Andalusia region of southern Spain. It is known for its refreshing and delicious taste, and it highlights the vibrant flavours of Spanish cuisine.

Many regions have their own variation but, typically, the four ingredients they have in common are: tomatoes, cucumbers, onions, and bell peppers. The Andalusian version also has ingredients like olives, sardines, egg, or tuna.

Pipirrana is a popular summer dish that is perfect on a hot day or when enjoyed as a side dish.

FOR THE SALAD

3 large ripe tomatoes, finely diced

1 cucumber, finely diced

1 green pepper, finely diced

1 red pepper, finely diced

1 red onion, finely diced

2 eggs, hard-boiled, chopped

1 x 150g tin of tuna

10-12 black olives

1 handful of fresh parsley, chopped, to garnish

FOR THE DRESSING

4 tbsp olive oil

2 tbsp white wine vinegar

1 clove of garlic, minced

1 tbsp lemon juice

½ tsp ground cumin

Salt and pepper, to taste

Combine the chopped ingredients with the tuna and olives in a large salad bowl.

Whisk the dressing ingredients together and toss with the salad. Cover and chill for 30 minutes before garnishing with chopped parsley and serving.

CORIANDER

THE CORIANDER CONNECTION

YEMEN, NORTH AFRICA, AND INDIA

Zhoug, Chermoula, and Indian chutneys (like my **Coriander and Kiwi Chutney**) are all vibrant, herb-based condiments that share a key commonality: their use of coriander. Despite originating from different regions – Zhoug from Yemen, Chermoula from North Africa, and chutney from India – they showcase the global appeal of coriander as a cuisine-defining ingredient.

The spread of coriander across Asia, Europe, and North Africa is largely attributed to ancient trade routes like the Silk Road. As it travelled along these routes, coriander became a staple ingredient in various cuisines, from India to the Mediterranean, and was highly valued for its versatility in cooking and its reputed medicinal properties.

India, North Africa, and the Middle East share a rich culinary tradition that heavily relies on the use of fresh herbs, garlic, and spices. These ingredients are fundamental in their cooking, particularly for marinades and dips. In India, fresh coriander, mint, garlic, and a variety of spices are blended into chutneys and used as marinades for meats and vegetables. Similarly, in North Africa, dishes like Chermoula feature a mix of fresh herbs, garlic, and spices as a marinade for fish or meat, while in the Middle East, Zhoug is a delicious and vibrant dip made with fresh herbs and garlic.

The inclusion of cumin in all three dips emphasises the shared culinary heritage of these regions and the influence of this spice in their respective cuisines. All three dips share a similar method of preparation, typically involving blending or processing the ingredients into a smooth paste or sauce. Across hundreds of miles of land and sea, it's hard to deny the amazing similarities in these countries' kitchens and how the use of coriander unites the dishes found on their tables.

ZHOUG

Yemen

Prep time: 10 minutes | Serves 4-6

Zhoug, also known as 'zhug' or 'skhug', is a vibrant and spicy coriander salsa that originated in Yemen and has gained popularity in Middle Eastern cuisine. It is made with fresh coriander, parsley, jalapenos, garlic, cardamom, cumin, and olive oil.

Zhoug is a versatile condiment. It can be served alongside falafel, shawarma, shakshuka, and a variety of other delicious dishes. It's also perfect as a marinade for meat or seafood, a dip for vegetables or pitta bread, or drizzled over grilled meat or roasted vegetables.

Zhoug can typically be stored in an airtight container in the refrigerator for up to 10 days.

I enjoy Zhoug as a dressing on a cucumber feta salad, spread on an egg sandwich, or as a topping for grilled corn.

35g fresh coriander
20g fresh parsley
2 green chillies
2 cloves of garlic, crushed
2 tbsp water
½ tsp ground cumin
¼ tsp ground coriander
¼ tsp ground cardamom
¼ tsp salt

Pinch of sugar, to taste
3 tbsp olive oil
2 tbsp lemon juice

In a food processor or blender, combine the fresh coriander and parsley, green chillies, and crushed garlic. Blend with 2 tablespoons of water until it forms a thick paste, then add a little more water, if desired, to achieve a smooth, pourable sauce. Add the ground cumin and coriander, cardamom, salt, and sugar. Mix well, then add the olive oil, lemon juice and more water, if required. Taste and adjust the seasoning as needed, adding more salt, lemon juice, or chillies according to your preference.

This quantity should be sufficient for four to six people if used as a condiment or sauce. If used more generously, either as a marinade or a main dressing, it might serve closer to four people.

CHERMOULA
North Africa

Chermoula is a popular condiment and marinade in North African cuisine, particularly in Algeria, Libya, Morocco, and Tunisia. It is typically made with fresh herbs like parsley and or coriander, garlic, citrus, warm spices, and sometimes preserved lemons. The sauce is often used to flavour fish, seafood, meat, and vegetables, and is known for its tangy, rich, and herby flavour.

Chermoula is little like chimichurri, the Argentinian herb sauce, as both use olive oil, fresh herbs, garlic, and red pepper flakes. Chermoula, however, also includes cumin and coriander, giving it a unique flavour. Traditionally made with a pestle and mortar, it can also be quickly prepared in a food processor.

I use this in multiple ways: it can be drizzled over roasted veggies, used as a marinade for tofu, or added to a chickpea or bean stew for a little extra oomph.

1 tsp cumin seeds
50g fresh coriander
20g fresh parsley
4 cloves of garlic
1 tsp ground coriander
1 tsp smoked paprika
Salt and pepper, to taste
1 lemon, juiced
4 tbsp olive oil
1 preserved lemon, finely chopped
1 tbsp red wine vinegar (optional)

Toast the cumin seeds in a dry pan until the seeds begin to crackle and smell aromatic, then tip them into a mortar and grind roughly.

In a food processor, combine the coriander, parsley, garlic, ground cumin seeds, ground coriander, smoked paprika, salt, and black pepper. Add the lemon juice and olive oil and blend until the mixture is smooth but still has some texture.

Add the preserved lemon and red wine vinegar, if using, and pulse a few times to incorporate. Taste and adjust the seasoning if necessary, adding more salt, pepper, or lemon juice as desired. Use immediately or store in an airtight container in the refrigerator for up to 1 week.

CORIANDER KIWI CHUTNEY

India

Prep time: 10 minutes | Serves 4-6

Coriander chutney is a vibrant and zesty condiment that forms an essential part of Indian cuisine. It is made by blending fresh coriander leaves with salt, ginger, green chillies, and sometimes grated coconut. It is incredibly versatile and pairs well with a variety of dishes, from samosas and pakoras to grilled meats and sandwiches.

I have made this chutney with kiwi fruit to add a sweet tanginess. I often use this chutney to make a Hariyali or green tofu stir fry, but it's also perfect on roasted veggies, or spread over toasted bagels and cream cheese.

1 bunch of fresh coriander

1 kiwi, peeled and roughly chopped

1-2 green chillies, chopped

2 cloves of garlic

2-3 tbsp water (adjust as needed)

2 tbsp lemon juice

½ tsp ground cumin; or ½ tsp cumin seeds, toasted and ground

½ tsp sugar

Salt, to taste

In a blender or food processor, combine the coriander, kiwi, green chillies, and garlic. Blend until you achieve a smooth, thick paste, adding water as needed until you reach the desired consistency.

Add the lemon juice, cumin, sugar, and salt. Mix well and adjust the seasoning the taste. This chutney can be stored in the fridge in an airtight container for a week.

COCONUT

GLOBAL COCONUT DELIGHTS

A TRIO OF RECIPES FROM INDONESIA, KENYA, AND INDIA

Coconut is a popular and widely used ingredient in India, Indonesia, and Kenya, deeply embedded in the culinary traditions of these regions. Its widespread use is largely due to the coconut's adaptability to tropical climates. The historical trade routes across the Indian Ocean facilitated the exchange of goods, including coconuts, and cultural practices among these regions. As a result, coconut became an essential part of the local cuisines, used in various forms such as coconut milk, oil, and grated coconut, and enriching dishes with its unique flavour. All three regions use grated coconut in a variety of dishes, from savoury curries to sweet desserts. Migrants and traders brought their culinary traditions with them, incorporating coconuts into local cuisines and adapting recipes to include native ingredients.

Tante Noni's Vegetable Coconut Stew is an example of the historical culinary connection between India and Indonesia that dates back to the early centuries of the Common Era, particularly around the first century CE. This dish highlights how Indian spices like turmeric and cumin, introduced through ancient trade routes, have been integrated into local cooking methods, resulting in a rich and flavourful curry that is a staple in Indonesian households. The influence of Indian culture and cuisine was further solidified between the 4th and 15th centuries, a period during which Hinduism and Buddhism spread to Indonesia, as evidenced by the ancient temples and inscriptions. This and other dishes, like Rendang and Gulai, feature slow-cooked meat in coconut milk and a blend of spices, reflecting both Indian and local flavours and techniques.

My recipe for **Mombasa Coconut Chutney** is a result of the Indian diaspora bringing their culinary traditions to East Africa, integrating them into Swahili cuisine, and popularising coconut chutney in Mombasa. Mombasa, as part of the Swahili Coast, has a rich history of interactions with various cultures, including Persian, Arab, and Indian traders. The Swahili culture itself is a blend of African, Arab, and Indian influences. During the 19th and early 20th centuries, there was significant migration from India to East Africa, including Mombasa, during the British colonial period. This historical connection, facilitated by centuries of trade and migration along the Indian Ocean, has led to a rich culinary fusion that is exemplified in this dish's use of green chillies, garlic, and coriander.

Coconut plays a significant role in Indian cuisine, particularly in the southern states of Kerala, Tamil Nadu, and Karnataka. Its use in cooking has ancient roots, especially in tropical areas where it thrives. Over time, the use of coconut spread throughout India and became a staple ingredient in many regional cuisines. Culturally, coconut holds religious significance as it is considered auspicious and is often used in Hindu rituals and ceremonies as a symbol of purity and prosperity.

Coconut is wonderfully versatile, perfect for both sweet and savoury dishes. I'm sharing a recipe for **Coconut Ladoos**, which are delicious, sweet balls made from coconut, milk and sugar. These ladoos are a popular Indian treat, offering a sweet, nutty flavour that's perfect for celebrations or simply enjoying with a cup of tea.

TANTE NONI'S VEGETABLE COCONUT STEW

Indonesia

Prep time: 20 minutes | Cooking time: 40 minutes | Serves 4

This dish, also called Sayur Lodeh, is a traditional Indonesian vegetable stew. This dish is made with a variety of vegetables cooked in a savoury coconut broth and flavoured with aromatic spices. The turmeric adds a warm, earthy note and a lovely yellow hue, while the ginger and lemongrass impart a fragrant, citrusy aroma. This is typically served with steamed rice or noodles.

There are many variations of this recipe, and this one is from my friend Janti, who has Indonesian heritage. A big thank you to her for sharing her Tante (Aunt) Noni's recipe, hence the name of this dish. I love cooking from family recipes because they make the dish so special and add a personal touch that you can't find anywhere else.

3 tbsp coriander seeds

1 tbsp cumin seeds

3 tbsp desiccated coconut

2 dried red chillies

2 tsp sugar

4 tbsp vegetable oil

1 onion, finely chopped

1 tbsp ginger paste

1 tbsp garlic paste

1 tsp curry powder

1 tsp turmeric

500ml water

200ml coconut milk

1 lemongrass stalk, bruised/crushed

3-4 dry pandan leaves

50g carrots, cut into 1-inch chunks

50g potatoes, parboiled, cut into 1-inch chunks

50g pumpkin, cut into 1-inch chunks

50g mooli (daikon radish), cut into 1-inch chunks

50g green beans cut into 1-inch chunks

50g tomatoes cut into 1-inch chunks

20g ball of tamarind, soaked in 3 tbsp of warm water for 15 minutes, pulp extracted

Salt, to taste

Dry roast the coriander seeds, cumin seeds, desiccated coconut, and red chillies in a small pan. Allow to cool before grinding with the sugar, then set aside.

Heat the oil in a wok, then add the onions and sauté on a high heat for few minutes. Add the ginger and garlic pastes and cook on a medium heat for 10 minutes until browned. Add the ground spices and sugar along with the curry powder, turmeric, and water. Mix well and cook for 3 to 4 minutes.

Add the coconut milk, lemongrass and pandan leaves, and simmer on a low heat for 5 minutes. Then, add the vegetables and tamarind pulp and season with salt. Cover and cook on a medium heat until the vegetables are cooked al dente, about 12 to 15 minutes. Add extra water, if necessary, and season to taste. Serve hot with rice or noodles.

NOTE

This curry can be made with any vegetables, just remember they need to be al dente and not mushy.

BINA'S MOMBASA COCONUT CURRY

Kenya

Prep time: 10 minutes | Cooking time: 10 minutes | Serves 4

Mombasa Coconut Chutney is a popular condiment from Mombasa, Kenya, which is often used in East African cuisine. Made from grated coconut and blended with ginger, garlic, chilli, and coriander, this chutney is well balanced with a touch of lemon juice or vinegar for acidity and a pinch of sugar for sweetness. It has a creamy yet slightly chunky texture and a spicy and somewhat sweet flavour.

This versatile chutney pairs well with fish and can be enjoyed with any savoury snack or used as a spread for sandwiches. Thank you, Bina, for sharing this amazing Mombasa Coconut Chutney recipe with me; it's been the perfect partner to the bhajiyas and endless conversations we've had at your place.

75g desiccated coconut

1 bunch of fresh coriander

2 green chillies, roughly chopped

1 clove of garlic, peeled

½ thumb of ginger, peeled and roughly chopped

1 small, raw mango

1 tbsp lime or lemon juice

¼ tsp ground cumin

Salt, to taste

200ml water

½ tsp sugar

Add the coconut, coriander (leaves and stems), green chillies, garlic, ginger, raw mango, lime or lemon juice, ground cumin, and salt in a food processor. Add water and blend all the ingredients together until smooth, adding a little extra water, if needed, to achieve the desired consistency.

Add the sugar and season the chutney to taste with more sugar, salt, or lime/lemon juice as needed.

COCONUT LADOOS

India

Prep time: 10 minutes | Cooking time: 40 minutes | Makes 12

Coconut ladoos, or nariyal laddu, are traditional Indian sweets made with coconut and sugar. They are often lightly flavoured with ground cardamom or rose water, and their soft, melt-in-the-mouth texture make them a favourite treat during festivals and celebrations.

These ladoos are a big hit every time I make them, whether at home or for an event. Their delightfully sweet, aromatic flavours and soft texture never fail to impress, and they have become a staple at every festival in my home, earning rave reviews from family and guests alike.

75g desiccated coconut, plus 3 tbsp to decorate
340ml full fat milk
100g caster sugar

Dry fry 75g of desiccated coconut in a pan for couple of minutes until very light toasted or a creamy colour. Keep stirring to make sure the coconut doesn't burn or brown. Remove and set aside.

Add the milk to a large, heavy bottom pan and bring to the boil. Add the toasted coconut, stirring continuously for about 12 to 15 minutes until the milk evaporates and the mixture has thickened. Add the sugar and stir continuously over a low heat. The sugar will start to melt and thin the mixture, so keep stirring for 10 minutes until the moisture evaporates and the mixture turns crumbly. Remove from the heat and set aside to cool.

Lightly grease your hands with a little ghee or oil to prevent the mixture from sticking, then take a small portion of the mixture – around the size of a walnut – and shape into a ball. To do this, roll the portioned mixture between your palms to form a smooth, round ball, applying gentle pressure to ensure the mixture holds together. Repeat until you've used all the mixture (about 12 balls).

Gently roll each ladoo in the remaining 3 tablespoons of coconut until each ball is evenly coated. Ensure the entire surface of the ladoo is covered for that extra touch of flavour and texture. Serve room temperature or slightly chilled.

NOTE

You can add a quarter of a teaspoon of ground cardamom or half a teaspoon of rose water to the mixture after it has cooked for extra flavour.

RADIKAL RECIPES
FLAVOURS & FUN UNLEASHED

This collection features recipes developed by combining various cuisines and flavours to create fun fusion dishes. As a flavour enthusiast, I love exploring and crafting dishes with my own unique twist. Fusion need not be confusion; it's thrilling to innovate by adding flavourful twists to existing recipes or by experimenting with new combinations. Some recipes are subtle, while others are bold and dramatic.

I would like to introduce the concept of Desi flavours in this context. Desi flavour refers to the distinctive taste and aromatic qualities of traditional South Asian cuisine, particularly from India, Pakistan, Bangladesh, and the surrounding regions. It is characterised by the use of a variety of spices, herbs, and ingredients native to these areas. Desi flavour is known for its bold, complex, and often spicy taste profiles. The warmth of cardamom, the earthiness of cumin, the brightness of turmeric, and the heat of chilli peppers are just a few examples of the diverse elements that come together in Desi cuisine. In essence, Desi flavours encapsulate the diverse cultural influences and regional nuances that have shaped South Asian cuisine, offering a feast for the senses that is both inviting and unforgettable.

In some of my recipes, in my quest to create new flavour combinations, I have taken traditional recipes and added a 'Desi twist'. For example, I add a curry leaf tadka to a tomato burrata salad or introduce Indian spices to the Spanish tortilla.

I came across the idea of adapting recipes to cultural tastes and giving them a twist when I arrived in the UK from India almost 27 years ago. I saw examples like masala baked beans and spicy pastas, which inspired me to experiment with fusion cuisine. Over time, my flavour guru, Yotam Ottolenghi, took me on a different journey, opening a whole new world of exciting flavours to enjoy. His innovative approach to combining diverse culinary traditions has greatly influenced my own cooking, encouraging me to explore and create unique dishes that blend traditional recipes with new, vibrant tastes.

I do hope you enjoy my collection of Radikal Recipes. Each dish is crafted with a passion for bold flavours and creative twists, and I encourage you to experiment with them. Feel free to add your own personal touch to these recipes and make them your own. I would love to hear about your culinary adventures and the unique variations you come up with, so please share your experiences with me. Happy cooking!

AVOCADO PAPDI CHAAT

Prep time: 15 minutes | Cooking time: 15 minutes | Serves 4-6

Avocado Papdi Chaat is a contemporary Indian tapas dish that brings a modern twist to the classic chaat concept, a beloved Indian street food. Papdi is a crispy, round, deep fried dough wafer made from refined flour, and it's commonly used as a base or topping in various Indian chaat dishes.

This innovative dish combines the creamy richness of avocado with the traditional crispiness of the papdi. It is topped with tangy tamarind chutney, spicy green chutney, and a sprinkle of chaat masala. Fresh herbs and pomegranate seeds add a burst of colour and flavour, making this chaat a perfect blend of textures and tastes.

1 packet of papdi discs (shop-bought, about 20 pieces)

FOR THE TOPPING

2 avocados, chopped into small pieces

1 small red onion, finely chopped

1 tomato, finely chopped

2 tbsp pomegranate seeds

1 green chilli, finely chopped

1 handful of coriander leaves, finely chopped

1 lime, juiced

1 tsp chaat masala or mango powder

1 tbsp tamarind chutney (shop-bought or homemade)

3 tbsp boondi or sev to garnish (shop-bought, see notes)

In a large bowl, combine the topping ingredients, except the boondi/sev. To assemble, spread the papdi on a serving tray and top each papdi with the tangy avocado mix. Finish with a sprinkling of the boondi or sev and serve.

NOTE

Boondi are small crispy balls made with gram flour, and sev are thin crispy strands that are also made from gram flour. They can be found in most Indian supermarkets and make a delicious crunchy topping to dishes.

BABY JACKET SPUDS WITH CREAM CHEESE AND CHILLI THECHA

Prep time: 15 minutes | Cooking time: 1 hour | Serves 6-8

This dish puts a 'radikal' twist on the traditional baked spud and cheese canapé by adding a spicy, aromatic Maharashtrian chilli and peanut chutney. The cream cheese blends seamlessly with the green chilli thecha, delivering a bold kick to each bite. Green thecha is a traditional spicy condiment from Maharashtra, India, that's made from fresh green chillies, peanuts, garlic, and cumin seeds. The tender baby potatoes serve as the perfect base, balancing the heat while adding a delightfully soft texture. This innovative canapé marries familiar comfort with an exciting burst of Indian-inspired flavours, making it a standout appetiser for any occasion.

500g baby new potatoes

2 tbsp olive oil

2 tbsp rock salt

3 tbsp unsalted peanuts, skinless

1 tbsp vegetable oil

10 green chillies, chopped

8-10 cloves of garlic, chopped

Salt and pepper, to taste

100g cream cheese

3 tbsp chives, finely chopped

1 tbsp red chilli flakes

Preheat the oven to 200°c, then prick the potatoes with a fork, rub with the oil, and toss with rock salt. Arrange on a baking sheet and bake for 35 minutes until golden and tender. Remove from the oven and allow to cool.

Meanwhile, prepare the thecha. Heat a dry pan on a medium heat, then add the raw peanuts and toast them for 3 to 4 minutes, stirring continuously. Once lightly blistered, set aside.

In the same pan, add the vegetable oil, chopped green chillies, and garlic. Sauté for about 6 to 8 minutes. Add the toasted peanuts and sauté for another 2 minutes. Let the sautéed mixture cool down, then transfer to a pestle and mortar (or electric grinder) and pound or grind the mixture to a coarse texture. Add salt and pepper to taste and mix well. Stir the pounded thecha through the cream cheese until fully combined.

Use a small, sharp knife to cut a circle out of the top of the potatoes; it should be slightly cone-shaped, creating a well for the thecha cheese filling to sit in. Spoon the filling into the potatoes and scatter with the chives and red chilli flakes.

BUCATINI TUNA MASALA WITH PEAS

Prep time: 15 minutes | Cooking time: 30 minutes | Serves 2

This pasta dish is a delightful fusion of Indo-Italian flavours. It combines the robust, spicy notes of Indian masala with hearty bucatini pasta and tender tuna. The Indian spices used in this dish create a unique flavour profile that is rich and aromatic without being overly chilli hot. Fragrant spices like cumin, coriander, turmeric and garam masala add depth and warmth to the dish, enhancing the natural flavours of the tuna and pasta. These spices provide a complex blend of earthy, savoury and slightly sweet notes, delivering a delightful and balanced taste experience that showcases the harmonious blend of Indian and Italian culinary traditions.

200g bucatini pasta

3 tbsp olive oil

1 onion, finely chopped

1 tsp ginger, grated

1 tsp garlic, grated

½ tin of tomatoes (200g)

1 tsp turmeric

1 tsp ground coriander

1 tsp ground cumin

½ tsp garam masala

2-3 green chillies, chopped (optional)

Salt, to taste

250ml water (adjust as needed)

1 x 145g tin of tuna, drained

80g frozen peas, thawed

15g black olives, sliced

1 tbsp capers (optional)

2 tbsp cream cheese (I like to use garlic cream cheese)

1 lemon, juiced

1 handful of fresh coriander leaves, to garnish

Fried onions, to garnish (optional)

Parmesan cheese, grated, to garnish

Boil the pasta in salted water until al dente (usually a couple of minutes less than the packet instructions).

Heat the olive oil in a pan, add the chopped onions, and sauté for 5 minutes until golden brown. Add the grated ginger and garlic and cook for another 5 minutes on a medium heat. Add the tomatoes and cook for a couple of minutes, then add the ground spices, green chillies and salt. Mix well and cook for a few minutes, adding a little water if you find the sauce is too thick.

Add the tuna to the pan and cook for 2 to 3 minutes before adding the peas, olives and capers. Add a little more water, if required, to reach the desired consistency (it should have a reasonably thick texture). Cover and cook for 5 minutes on a medium heat.

Stir through the cream cheese and bucatini until the pasta is well coated. Add a squeeze of lemon juice and garnish with coriander leaves and crispy fried onions. Finish with a generous grating of parmesan cheese and serve immediately.

CHARGRILLED ASPARAGUS TOPPED WITH ANDHRA-STYLE PODI (DRY PEANUT CHUTNEY)

Prep time: 30 minutes | Cooking time: 10 minutes | Serves 2-3

This dish is a vibrant fusion of British and Indian flavours featuring chargrilled asparagus topped with a dry and crunchy peanut-garlic chutney, known as podi. A podi is a traditional South Indian spice powder used as a condiment or seasoning in various dishes. It is made by dry roasting a combination of ingredients such as lentils, spices, and nuts or dried herbs, and then grinding them into a fine or coarse powder.

This podi is prepared Andhra-style, a version known for its nuttier and spicier flavour. This recipe uses peanuts instead of the classic lentils, adding a unique twist. This differs from Tamil podi, which typically includes curry leaves and asafoetida, with less emphasis on sesame seeds and garlic.

These tender, smoky asparagus spears are perfectly complemented by this aromatic podi, and this recipe is ideal as an appetiser or a side dish.

250g asparagus, woody ends snapped off
20g butter
1 lemon, juiced

FOR THE PODI MASALA

150g unsalted peanuts, skinless
15g sesame seeds
½ tsp oil
1 tsp cumin seeds
1 tsp coriander seeds
5 dried red chillies, crushed
8-10 cloves of garlic
Salt, to taste

To make the podi masala, toast the peanuts and sesame seeds in a dry pan for 4 to 5 minutes, then set aside to cool. Shake frequently to prevent burning.

Heat a pan on a medium heat and add the oil, cumin seeds, coriander seeds, and red chillies and sauté the spices for 3 to 4 minutes, stirring continuously to prevent burning. Transfer to a plate and allow to cool.

Combine the toasted spices, nuts and sesame seeds, garlic cloves, and a pinch of salt, then coarsely blend. You can use an electric grinder or a pestle and mortar. The mix should have a granular texture.

Cook the asparagus in butter on a griddle pan on high heat for 4 to 5 minutes. The asparagus should be cooked yet retain a bite.

Place the asparagus on a platter, sprinkle the podi mix on top, and finish with a squeeze of lemon juice. This dish is best served warm.

COCONUT SAMBAL SPAGHETTI

Prep time: 15 minutes | Cooking time: 25 minutes | Serves 2-3

Inspired by the vibrant flavours of Indonesian Tomato and Coconut Sambal, this innovative recipe transforms a traditional condiment into a delicious pasta sauce.

Sambal is known for its versatility and unique flavour profile. It typically includes ground or crushed ingredients like chillies, garlic, ginger, shallots, tomatoes, shrimp paste and various other spices. There are numerous regional variations of sambal across Indonesia, Malaysia, Singapore, and other Southeast Asian countries. The term is spelled both 'sambal' and 'sambol', depending on where it is from. Sambal is commonly used in Indonesian and Malaysian cuisine, whereas the term 'sambol' is often used in Sri Lankan cuisine to describe a similar type of condiment.

200g spaghetti

4 tbsp vegetable oil

1 large onion, thinly sliced

10-12 curry leaves

1 tbsp ginger, grated

1 tbsp garlic, chopped

2-3 green chillies, chopped (optional)

1 tsp turmeric

1 tsp ground coriander

½ tsp ground cumin

Salt, to taste

400g cherry tomatoes (200g whole; 200g halved)

200ml coconut milk

250ml water (adjust as needed)

1 lime, juiced

1 handful of fresh basil leaves, to garnish

2 tbsp peanuts, toasted and lightly crushed

Boil the spaghetti in salted water and cook until al dente (usually a couple of minutes less than the packet instructions).

Meanwhile, heat the oil in a pan and sauté the sliced onions and curry leaves for 6 to 8 minutes until golden-brown. Add the ginger and garlic and mix well before adding the chopped green chillies, ground spices and salt. Mix well and cook for a few minutes, adding 2 tablespoons of water if you find the mixture needs thinning.

Add the tomatoes, then cover and cook on a medium heat for 8 minutes before adding the coconut milk and the water to make a smooth sauce. Add extra water, if required, to reach the desired consistency. Cover and cook for 3 to 4 minutes.

Add the lime juice and garnish with basil leaves before stirring the spaghetti through the sauce. Sprinkle some toasted peanuts and serve hot.

KESAR BOONDI ARANCINI

Prep time: 15 minutes, plus 1 hour 30 minutes chilling | Cooking time: 45 minutes | Makes 14-16

This is my Kesar Boondi Arancini - a unique fusion dish that combines the rich flavours of saffron with the traditional Italian arancini. These delightful arancini balls are infused with the delicate aroma of saffron (kesar), and each arancini ball features a crunchy filling of boondi – tiny, crispy chickpea flour pearls – mixed with fresh herbs. This unexpected filling adds a delightful texture contrast, making each bite an exciting and flavourful experience. This recipe is perfect as an appetiser.

FOR THE RICE

1 tbsp vegetable oil

1 tbsp butter

1 onion, finely chopped

1 tbsp ginger, grated

1 tsp turmeric

1 tsp ground coriander

Salt, to taste

10-15 saffron threads, brewed in 2 tbsp warm water

1 lemon, juiced

600g cooked rice

FOR THE FILLING

50g paneer, grated

50g raisins

2 tbsp fresh coriander leaves, chopped

2 tbsp fresh dill leaves, chopped

30g boondi (shop-bought)

Salt, to taste

FOR THE COATING

2 tbsp cornflour, mixed with 250ml water

2 eggs, beaten

200g fine breadcrumbs

Vegetable oil, to deep fry

Heat the oil and butter in a large pan, then add the onions and sauté for 3 to 4 minutes until light brown. Add the ginger and sauté for another 2 to 3 minutes before adding the turmeric, coriander and salt. Sauté for 2 to 3 minutes on a medium heat, then add the saffron and lemon juice and mix well. Add the cooked rice and mix well, then spread the mixture onto a large plate to cool for an hour.

To make the filling, combine the paneer, raisins, herbs and boondi, then season with salt.

To make the arancini, begin by taking a small spoonful of the flavoured rice and cupping it in the palm of your hand. Put a small amount of paneer filling in the centre and cover with the rice. Roll into a ball and set aside. Repeat with the remaining rice and filling to make approximately 15 arancini balls then chill in the fridge for 30 minutes.

Place the cornflour mix, beaten egg, and breadcrumbs in separate shallow bowls. Dip each arancini into the cornflour, followed by the eggs and finally, the breadcrumbs. Transfer to a tray and set aside.

Heat a good amount of vegetable oil in a pan ready to deep fry the arancini. Lower the coated rice balls into the oil in batches and cook for 8 to 10 minutes, or until golden-brown and melty in the centre. Serve warm with a chutney or sauce of your choice.

MARRY ME CHICKPEAS

Prep time: 10 minutes | Cooking time: 30 minutes | Serves 4

These are my Marry Me Chickpeas - the veggie dish that's stealing hearts everywhere! Inspired by the famous Marry Me Chicken, this delightful creation features chickpeas cooked in a creamy Tuscan-style tomato sauce with sun-dried tomatoes, garlic, and a medley of aromatic herbs. Whether you are planning a romantic dinner or just a cosy night in, Marry Me Chickpeas promise to deliver a taste experience so good you might just pop the question!

Marry Me Chickpeas can be served with crusty bread, rice, pasta, roasted or steamed vegetables, a fresh salad, or even jacket potatoes, making it a versatile and satisfying meal option.

2 tbsp butter

1 onion, finely chopped

6-7 cloves of garlic, minced

4 tbsp sun-dried tomato paste

150ml water (adjust as needed)

2 x 400g tins of chickpeas, drained

1 tsp oregano

1 tsp red chilli flakes, plus extra to garnish

Salt and pepper, to taste

6 tbsp sun-dried tomatoes (jarred), chopped

12-15 fresh basil leaves, plus extra to garnish

2 tbsp crème fraîche

3 tbsp parmesan cheese, grated

Heat the butter in a pan and sauté the onions for 5 minutes until golden-brown. Add the garlic and cook for another 3 to 4 minutes on a medium heat. Add the sun-dried tomato paste, mix well, then add 50ml of water.

Add the drained chickpeas and remaining 100ml of water and simmer on a medium heat for 5 minutes. Add the oregano, red chilli flakes, salt, and chopped sun-dried tomatoes. Cook for 2 to 3 minutes before adding half the fresh basil leaves.

Mash some of the chickpeas with a potato masher to add a creaminess to the sauce's texture. Season to taste with salt and pepper, then cover and simmer for 10 minutes. Add more water, if required, to reach the desired consistency, then stir in the crème fraîche and remaining basil leaves and mix well.

Finish with grated parmesan and some extra basil leaves and chilli flakes.

MUSHROOM DOPYAZA CROSTINI

Prep time: 15 minutes | Cooking time: 30 minutes | Serves 6-8 (as an appetiser)

Mushroom Dopyaza Crostini is a contemporary twist on the classic Indian dopyaza recipe, traditionally known for its generous use of onions cooked in rich, aromatic spices. This innovative appetiser features mushrooms sautéed with caramelised onions, ginger and cinnamon served on crispy crostini.

The fusion of traditional Indian flavours with the delightful crunch of toasted bread creates a unique and delectable bite-sized treat, perfect for parties and get-togethers.

For added flavour, you can spread some green chutney or cream cheese on the crostini before adding the Mushroom Dopyaza topping.

2 tbsp butter

2 medium onions, finely chopped

1 tsp ginger, grated

400g mushrooms, finely chopped

1 tsp garam masala

½ tsp ground cinnamon

1 tsp red chilli flakes

Salt, to taste

1 baguette, cut into half-inch slices

Olive oil, to drizzle

2 tbsp fresh coriander leaves, finely chopped, to garnish

Melt the butter in a large heavy-bottomed pan over a medium heat. Add the chopped onions and fry for 5 minutes until golden-brown. Add the grated ginger and cook for a further 2 minutes.

Add the mushrooms and stir fry over a high heat for 7 to 8 minutes or until the moisture from the mushrooms has evaporated. Add the garam masala, cinnamon, chilli flakes and salt, then cook for 2 minutes before setting aside.

Brush each slice of baguette with olive oil. Grill in the oven for 15 minutes until nicely toasted. Place a generous topping of the mushroom mix onto the baguette and garnish with coriander leaves. Serve warm.

SAAG PANEER OMELETTE

Prep time: 15 minutes | Cooking time: 20 minutes | Serves 2-3

This Saag Paneer Omelette is a delightful fusion of Indian flavours and classic breakfast fare. It's perfect for enjoying as a main meal or a hearty brunch. This recipe features a fluffy omelette filled with a mildly spiced savoury mixture of Indian cheese (paneer) and spinach, cooked with aromatic spices to create a flavourful masala filling.

6 eggs

½ tsp turmeric

Salt and pepper, to taste

100g paneer, grated

200g spinach, very finely chopped (or blended)

1 medium onion, finely chopped

2 cloves of garlic, minced

1 large tomato, finely chopped

2 green chillies, chopped (optional)

1 tsp ground coriander

4 tbsp vegetable oil

Whisk the eggs, turmeric, salt, and pepper together in a large bowl until well combined.

To prepare the filling, mix the grated paneer with the chopped spinach, onions, garlic, tomato, chillies, coriander, and a pinch of salt. Heat 2 tablespoons of oil in a pan and sauté the spinach and paneer mix for 5 minutes, then set aside.

To prepare the omelette, place a non-stick pan over a medium heat, add the remaining oil, then pour the egg mixture into the pan.

Let the eggs cook, undisturbed, for about 4 to 5 minutes until the edges start to set. Then, gently tilt the pan and use a spatula to lift the edges of the omelette, allowing the uncooked eggs to flow underneath. Cook for 3 to 4 minutes before turning over to cook the other side for another 4 minutes.

Put the spinach paneer filling on one half of the omelette and fold the omelette in half using a spatula. Cook for another minute to warm the filling through, then serve warm.

TOMATO BURRATA SALAD WITH CURRY LEAF TADKA

Prep time: 10 minutes | Cooking time: 30 minutes | Serves 4

Experience a delightful fusion of Italian and Indian culinary traditions with this Tomato Burrata Salad enhanced by a curry leaf tadka.

The highlight of this dish is the Indian tadka, a tempering technique used to elevate the flavours of spices. Here, the tadka is made by sizzling mustard seeds and aromatic curry leaves in hot oil until they pop and release their lemony and nutty aromas. This fragrant mixture is then drizzled over the burrata, infusing it with a delightful blend of flavours that perfectly complement the mild, creamy cheese and the tangy sweetness of the tomatoes.

200g cherry tomatoes

5 cloves of garlic, finely chopped

3 tbsp olive oil

Salt, to taste

2-3 green chillies, finely chopped (optional)

1 burrata

FOR THE TADKA

2 tbsp olive oil

1 tsp black mustard seeds

2-3 cloves of garlic, chopped

8-10 curry leaves

Preheat the oven to 200°c and line a small baking sheet with parchment paper. Wash the tomatoes well and pat dry, then scatter them over the baking sheet and top with the garlic, olive oil and salt. Bake for 20 minutes.

Remove from the oven, mix the chillies through the tomatoes, then spread them on a platter and place the burrata in the centre. To make the tadka, heat the oil in a small pan, then add the black mustard seeds and wait for them to crackle and pop. Add the chopped garlic and curry leaves and fry for a few seconds until lightly crisp. Pour the hot spiced oil on top of the burrata, then serve with some crusty bread.

TORTILLA DE PATATAS WITH CUMIN AND PEAS

Prep time: 15 minutes | Cooking time: 40 minutes | Serves 4-6

This is my recipe for an Indo-Spanish tortilla! Inspired by the traditional Spanish tortilla my wonderful Spanish mother-in-law taught me to make, this version uses Indian spices and peas to add a playful twist. Imagine the comforting layers of tender potatoes and onions but with a burst of cumin, coriander, and turmeric infusing each bite with aromatic warmth. The addition of green peas brings a pop of colour and sweetness, making this dish not only delicious but visually stunning. Perfect for brunch, lunch, or part of a tapas, this Indo-Spanish tortilla is a global culinary adventure on a plate!

150ml olive oil
1 tsp cumin seeds
6-8 cloves of garlic, finely chopped
4 onions, peeled and sliced
5 medium potatoes, peeled and thinly sliced
150g frozen peas
1 tsp turmeric
1 tsp ground coriander
Salt and pepper, to taste
6 eggs, beaten

Heat 50ml of olive oil in a large frying pan over a low-medium heat and add the cumin seeds, garlic, and onions. Sauté for 5 minutes before adding the sliced potatoes. Mix well, cover, and cook on a low heat for 10 minutes.

Stir in the peas, turmeric, coriander, salt and pepper, then cover and continue to cook for about 15 minutes, stirring occasionally. When mixing, try to mash the potatoes and onion mixture thoroughly to break down any larger lumps of potatoes. Once the potatoes are cooked, transfer to a bowl and allow to cool.

Pour the beaten eggs over the cooled potato and pea mixture and stir to combine. Add the remaining oil to the pan, turn to a medium heat, and add the egg and potato mixture. Turn the heat to low and cook for 8 minutes until the egg has firmed up. Gently run a spatula around the edges to prevent sticking.

To flip the tortilla, cover the pan with a large plate and invert quickly so the tortilla falls onto the plate. Slide the tortilla back into the pan to cook the other side for another 6 to 8 minutes. Check the tortilla is cooked, then remove from the pan and allow to rest. The tortilla can be served warm or at room temperature.

NOTE

The cooking time will vary depending on the depth of your pan and the amount of heat from your cooker, so use your best judgement before flipping. If this is the first time you've made a tortilla, you might want to practise the flipping action with a plate and an empty pan first!

PANTRY ESSENTIALS

Here's a list of ingredients you'll always find in my kitchen cupboards – they're in many of my recipes, too.

I keep small quantities of each, but I try to keep them stocked up to avoid constant trips to the supermarket. Having these essentials on hand also saves money and helps you plan your meals better.

GROUND SPICES

Black Pepper: A sharp and mildly spicy powder that adds heat to a wide range of dishes.

Coriander: A mild, citrusy spice with a slightly sweet and lemony flavour. Perfect for curries and spice blends.

Cumin: A warm, slightly smoky spice with a pungent aroma, commonly used in Indian, Middle Eastern, and Mexican cuisines.

Curry Powder: A blend of spices, including turmeric, cumin, coriander, and chilli powder, used in various cuisines to add a robust and aromatic flavour.

Garam Masala: A blend of ground spices like cumin, coriander, cardamom, and cinnamon, used in Indian cooking to add warmth and complexity.

Spanish Smoked Paprika: A rich, smoky spice made from dried and smoked red peppers, adding a deep flavour to dishes like paella and stews.

Tandoori Masala: A blend of spices, including cumin, coriander, garlic, and paprika, used in Indian cuisine to marinate meats and vegetables.

Turmeric: A bright yellow spice with a warm, earthy flavour. It's often used for colour and depth in curries and stews.

WHOLE SPICES

Cardamom Pods: Green or black pods with a sweet, floral aroma and a complex flavour, often used in Indian and Middle Eastern dishes.

Cinnamon Sticks: Whole, aromatic sticks that release a sweet, woody flavour when simmered in liquids or ground fresh.

Cloves: Small, nail-shaped buds with a strong, sweet, and slightly bitter flavour.

Cumin Seeds: Small brown seeds with a warm, earthy flavour, often toasted or fried to release their aromatic oils.

Fennel Seeds: Small green seeds with a sweet, liquorice-like flavour, commonly used in Italian, Indian, and Middle Eastern cuisines to add a sweet and aromatic note.

Fenugreek Seeds: Small golden seeds with a slightly bitter, nutty flavour, used in spice blends and curries.

Mustard Seeds: Tiny seeds that come in yellow, brown, or black varieties, offering a pungent, slightly bitter taste when toasted.

Nigella (Onion) Seeds: Small black seeds with a slightly bitter, peppery taste, often used in Indian and Middle Eastern cooking.

Whole Peppercorns: Black, white, green, or pink peppercorns with varying flavours, ranging from sharp and pungent to mildly sweet. Grind them fresh for maximum flavour.

NUTS AND SEEDS

Almonds: Crunchy nuts with a slightly sweet flavour, often used in baking, cooking, and as a healthy snack.

Cashews: Creamy, buttery nuts with a mildly sweet flavour, commonly used in both savoury dishes and desserts, as well as for making dairy-free cream sauces.

Peanuts: Crunchy with a rich, nutty flavour, often used in snacks, desserts, and savoury dishes.

Pistachios: Small green nuts with a distinctive sweet and slightly earthy flavour, perfect for snacking, baking, and adding texture to dishes.

Sesame Seeds: Tiny, oval seeds with a mild, nutty flavour, often used in baking, cooking, and as a garnish.

SAUCES AND VINEGARS

Balsamic Vinegar: A dark, richly flavoured vinegar made from grape must; used to enhance salads, marinades, and glazes with its sweet and tangy taste.

Fish Sauce: A pungent, salty sauce made from fermented fish, widely used in Southeast Asian cooking to provide depth and a robust umami flavour to dishes.

Malt Vinegar: A tangy, dark vinegar made from malted barley, commonly used to add a sharp, robust flavour to savoury dishes like fish and chips.

Oyster Sauce: A thick, dark sauce made from oyster extracts, sugar, and salt, adding a rich, salty-sweet flavour and glossy finish to stir fries and marinades.

Red Chilli Sauce: A spicy, tangy condiment made from red chillies, vinegar, and garlic, perfect for adding heat to dishes; widely available in supermarkets.

Rice Vinegar: A mild and slightly sweet vinegar made from fermented rice, often used in Asian cooking for dressings, marinades, and sushi rice.

Soy Sauce: A condiment made from fermented soybeans, available in both dark and light varieties, adding a salty, umami flavour to dishes.

MISCELLANEOUS

Coconut Milk: A creamy, dairy-free liquid made from grated coconut flesh, used to add richness and subtle sweetness to soups, curries, and desserts.

Gochujang: A Korean red chilli paste with a sweet, spicy, and savoury flavour, used to add depth and heat to marinades, sauces, and stews.

Saffron: A prized crimson spice with an earthy, floral flavour and golden hue, used in rice dishes, stews, and desserts.

Sun-dried Tomatoes: Intensely flavoured tomatoes that are dried in the sun, offering a tangy, slightly sweet taste and chewy texture. Perfect for adding depth to salads, pastas, and sauces.

Tahini: A creamy paste made from ground sesame seeds, commonly used in Middle Eastern and Mediterranean dishes for its rich, nutty flavour.

Tamarind: A tangy, sour fruit pulp often used in Asian and Latin American cooking to add a tart, slightly sweet and tangy flavour to dishes.

HERBS (FRESH AND DRIED)

Basil: A fragrant herb with a sweet, slightly peppery flavour, commonly used in Italian and Thai dishes to add freshness and aroma to sauces, salads, and soups.

Bay Leaves: Dried leaves with a subtle, slightly floral flavour, used to add depth to soups, stews, and sauces.

Chives: A mild, onion-flavoured herb that adds a delicate touch to salads and soups. It can also be used as a garnish for various dishes.

Coriander: A bright, citrusy herb used in various cuisines for its fresh, zesty flavour that makes a great complement to salsas, curries, and salads.

Curry Leaf: Aromatic leaves with a slightly citrusy and nutty flavour, commonly used in Indian and Sri Lankan cuisine.

Dill: A feathery herb with a mild, slightly tangy flavour, often used in pickling, salads, and seafood dishes.

Kasuri Methi (Fenugreek Leaves): A dried herb with a slightly bitter, earthy flavour, often used in Indian and Pakistani cuisine to add depth and aroma.

Lemongrass: A fragrant herb with a fresh, lemony flavour, often used in Southeast Asian cooking to add a bright, citrusy note to soups and curries.

Mint: A refreshing herb with a cool, refreshing flavour, perfect for adding a burst of freshness to drinks, desserts, and savoury dishes.

Oregano: A pungent, earthy herb with a slightly bitter flavour, often used in Mediterranean dishes.

Parsley: A versatile herb with a clean, slightly peppery taste, used to garnish dishes and add freshness to soups, stews, and salads.

Thyme: An earthy, slightly minty herb often used in dried form to add depth to soups, stews, and roasted dishes.

Radhika 🄾 @radikalkitchen